MAZURIA

Bug River

Warsaw

Vistula River

GALICIA

TATRA MOUNTAINS

CARPATHIAN MOUNTAINS

SLOVAKIA

Budapest

ALFÖLD

Danube River

Tisza River

EASTERN EUROPE

CZECHOSLOVAKIA

HUNGARY

POLAND

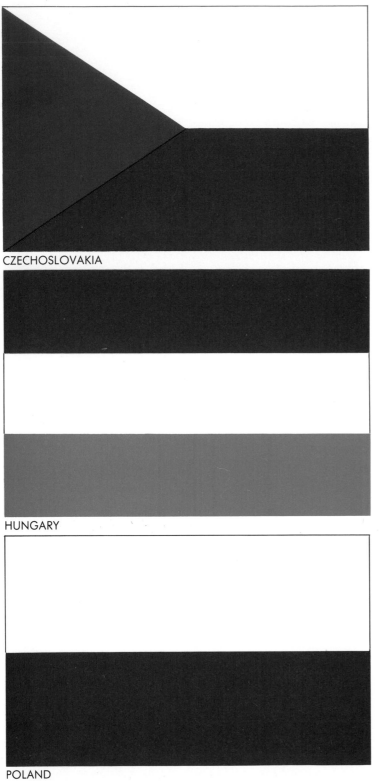

CZECHOSLOVAKIA

HUNGARY

POLAND

EASTERN EUROPE

By the Editors of Time-Life Books

TIME-LIFE BOOKS · ALEXANDRIA, VIRGINIA

Other Publications

MYSTERIES OF THE UNKNOWN
TIME FRAME
FIX IT YOURSELF
FITNESS, HEALTH & NUTRITION
SUCCESSFUL PARENTING
HEALTHY HOME COOKING
UNDERSTANDING COMPUTERS
THE ENCHANTED WORLD
THE KODAK LIBRARY OF
    CREATIVE PHOTOGRAPHY
GREAT MEALS IN MINUTES
THE CIVIL WAR
PLANET EARTH
COLLECTOR'S LIBRARY OF THE CIVIL WAR
THE EPIC OF FLIGHT
THE GOOD COOK
WORLD WAR II
HOME REPAIR AND IMPROVEMENT
THE OLD WEST

This volume is one in a series of books
describing countries of the world—their
natural resources, peoples, histories, economies and governments.

For information on and a full description of
any of the Time-Life Books series listed above,
please write:
Reader Information
Time-Life Customer Service
P.O. Box C-32068
Richmond, Virginia 23261-2068

Time-Life Books Inc.
is a wholly owned subsidiary of

TIME INCORPORATED

FOUNDER: HENRY R. LUCE 1898-1967

Editor-in-Chief: Henry Anatole Grunwald
Chairman and Chief Executive Officer: J. Richard Munro
President and Chief Operating Officer: N. J. Nicholas Jr.
Chairman of the Executive Committee: Ralph P. Davidson
Corporate Editor: Ray Cave
Executive Vice President, Books: Kelso F. Sutton
Vice President, Books: George Artandi

TIME-LIFE BOOKS INC.

EUROPEAN EDITOR: Kit van Tulleken
Assistant European Editor: Gillian Moore
Design Director: Ed Skyner
Photography Director: Pamela Marke
Chief of Research: Vanessa Kramer
Chief Sub-editor: Ilse Gray

LIBRARY OF NATIONS

Editorial Staff for *Eastern Europe*
Editor: Ellen Galford
Researcher: Mark Karras
Designer: Mary Staples
Sub-editor: Wendy Gibbons
Picture Department: Christine Hinze,
Peggy Tout
Editorial Assistant: Molly Oates

EDITORIAL PRODUCTION

Coordinator: Nikki Allen
Assistant: Maureen Kelly
Editorial Department: Theresa John,
Debra Lelliott

Contributors: The chapter texts were written by: Wind-
sor Chorlton, Judith Dempsey, Timothy Garton-Ash,
Frederic V. Grunfeld and Alan Lothian.

Assistant Editor for the U.S. edition: Barbara Fairchild
Quarmby

CONSULTANT

George Schöpflin lectures in Eastern
European Politics at the London School
of Economics and at the School of Slavonic and East European Studies at the
University of London. He has published
extensively on East-Central Europe and is
a frequent visitor to the area.

First Printing

Printed in U.S.A.
Published simultaneously in Canada.
School and library distribution by Silver Burdett
Company, Morristown, New Jersey.

TIME-LIFE is a trademark of Time Incorporated
U.S.A.

Library of Congress Cataloguing in Publication Data
Eastern Europe.
    (Library of nations)
    Bibliography: p.
    1. Europe, Eastern 2. Czechoslovakia.
3. Hungary. 4. Poland.
I. Time-Life Books. II. Series.
DJK9.E24 1987   947   87-10224
ISBN 0-8094-5152-2
ISBN 0-8094-5153-0 (lib. bdg.)

Cover: A steeply roofed wooden house,
constructed in the traditional style of the
górale, Poland's mountain dwellers, nestles
amid larch and spruce forests on the lower slopes of the High Tatra. The highest range
of the Western Carpathians, the Tatra Mountains dominate the border between Poland and
Czechoslovakia.

Front and back endpapers: A topographic map
showing the major rivers, plains, mountain
ranges and other natural features of Hungary,
Czechoslovakia and Poland appears on the
front endpaper; the back endpaper shows the
major cities and towns of these three Eastern
European countries.

CONTENTS

High-fliers in Hungary's burgeoning export trade, these handsome Emden geese have been raised for the delectation of Western palates. Hungary is the

EXPORTS EAST AND WEST

Founder members of Comecon—a trading bloc established in 1949 by the Soviet Union and the nations of Eastern Europe—Poland, Hungary and Czechoslovakia export most of their goods to the East. Since 1970, however, exports to the West have risen steadily, and as the chart above shows, recent trading patterns reflect each country's political and economic orientation. Comparatively liberal Hungary sends 1 truckload in 3 of its exports to Western Europe and the United States, while the more orthodox Czechoslovaks send only 1 truckload out of every 5½ to the West.

world's leading exporter of goose liver, most of it purchased by the French for transformation into pâté de foie gras.

BULWARKS OF CHRISTENDOM

Religious belief, denounced by Karl Marx as "the opium of the people," has been discouraged throughout Eastern Europe since the end of World War II. In the 1950s, it was dangerous to be a priest; and even in the 1980s, believers who practiced their faith openly could damage their careers.

Yet after 40 years of political suppression, the Roman Catholic Church in the late 1980s remained a powerful spiritual force. In Czechoslovakia and Hungary, up to 60 percent of the population is Catholic, although congregations are sometimes elderly and may gather in secret. In Poland, where piety goes hand in hand with patriotic fervor, 93 percent have been baptized into the Church. The inspiring quality of the Poles' faith was recognized in 1978, when Polish archbishop Karol Wojtyla was elected Pope John Paul II.

Their piety unquenched by a fierce Easter blizzard, thousands of devout Poles watch *The Way of the Cross,* **a Passion play. Each year it is performed at**

Kalwaria Zebrzydowska, near Kraków, by local farmers and monks from the monastery of St. Bernard.

The Soviet commander of the Warsaw Pact forces outshines his khaki-uniformed Hungarian colleague by sheer weight of medals as they review newly

AN ARMED ALLIANCE OF SOCIALIST STATES

Poland, Hungary and Czechoslovakia are all members of the Warsaw Pact, a mutual defense organization led by the Soviet Union, which also includes East Germany, Bulgaria and Rumania. Founded in 1955 to counter NATO in Europe, the pact coordinates national forces that, outside the U.S.S.R., total almost one million men, some 25,000 tanks and about 3,000 aircraft under a unified command structure. Exercises are conducted twice yearly, both to practice tactical maneuvers and to demonstrate to the West military readiness.

Soviet officers dominate the high command, thus enabling the Soviet Union to control its allies. The Soviet troops stationed in member countries—roughly 40,000 in Poland, 65,000 in Hungary and 80,000 in Czechoslovakia—are far better equipped than the national armies, and they are ready to intervene in their host countries' affairs when ordered. Soviet forces assigned to the Warsaw Pact helped crush the Hungarian uprising of 1956 and the Prague Spring of 1968; the imposition of martial rule in Poland in 1981 almost certainly preempted a third invasion.

commissioned officers on Constitution Day in Budapest.

LAND OWNERSHIP IN EASTERN EUROPE

4% — 77% | 6% 26% | 6% 30%
19% | 68% | 64%
POLAND | HUNGARY | CZECHOSLOVAKIA

● Private   ● State   ○ Cooperative

SHARING THE WEALTH OF THE LAND

At the end of World War II, the farmland of Eastern Europe was a mosaic of privately owned smallholdings, whose productivity was extremely low. Since 1945, all three countries have made strenuous efforts to improve yields by creating much larger farms under state or cooperative ownership. As the chart shows, their success has varied greatly. In Hungary and Czechoslovakia, two thirds of the land is now farmed cooperatively, with former owners sharing profits; state farms, with salaried workers, account for most of the remainder. But Poland has lagged behind, despite repeated government campaigns, and 77 percent of the country's farmland remains in private hands.

On a summer's evening, a horse-drawn plow carves a Polish hilltop into furrows while families tend their private vegetable plots. The traditional

pattern of ribbon-like fields, dating to medieval times, ensures that each farmer has an equal share of sunlight and fertile soil.

The golden light of dawn plays on Prague's most famous landmark: the dark twin spires of St. Vitus' Cathedral, rising above the massive Hradčany

Castle. The gray waters of the Vltava flow past the sleeping city, "a jewel," according to the poet Goethe, "in the country's crown of stone."

THREE VARIANTS
OF SOCIALISM

Carrying portraits of the founders of Communism—Marx, Lenin and Engels—uniformed Hungarian bus drivers swell a May Day parade through Budapest. Simultaneous marches take place throughout Eastern Europe on May 1, the major public holiday of the Communist bloc.

The peoples of Hungary, Czechoslovakia and Poland are still sometimes unpleasantly surprised to discover that their countries are designated as "Eastern Europe." Regarding themselves as an integral part of the cultural fabric of the Continent, they find the geographical qualifier demeaning. Did they not, after all, opt decisively for the West at an early stage in their histories by choosing Roman Catholicism over Eastern Orthodoxy as their national religions? And were they not for crucial centuries Western Europe's most important bulwark against tsarist Russia and Ottoman Turkey, the expanding empires of the East?

The unwelcome change in their geopolitical status dates from World War II. Beginning in 1939, Nazi Germany occupied or installed puppet regimes in all three countries—which were liberated by the Red Army at the end of the war. But the liberating forces stayed on, and at the Yalta and Potsdam conferences of 1945, the leaders of the Allied powers acknowledged Soviet military hegemony over all three as a *fait accompli*. Together with such culturally disparate bedfellows as East Germany, Rumania and Bulgaria, the three nations were then forcibly integrated into the Soviet bloc as satellite states, cut off from their Western European neighbors by the 870 miles of barbed wire, watchtowers, antitank ditches and mine fields that Sir Winston Churchill called the Iron Curtain. In the words of the Czech novelist Milan Kundera: "After 1945, the border between the two Europes shifted several hundred kilometers to the west, and several nations that had always considered themselves to be Western woke up to discover they were now in the East."

The term "Eastern Europe," as it is used in current parlance, dates from the late 1940s, when the powers in Moscow, with the support of local Communists, swept away the old orders of the three nations and replaced them with approximations of the Soviet political and economic system. Geographically, the term is hardly accurate. After all, the Czechoslovakian capital of Prague lies farther west than Vienna; and Budapest and Warsaw, the chief cities of Hungary and Poland, are closer to Berlin than they are to Moscow. But the term is now used not so much as a geographical definition as an ideological distinction. When Poland's Frédéric Chopin traveled from Warsaw to Paris to play his native mazurkas and polonaises for a French audience, and when Mozart made the trip to Prague to compose *Don Giovanni* and watch its first performance, neither man was conscious of crossing a major cultural boundary. Travelers making the same journeys in the 20th century, however, are aware that they are crossing a great divide, exchanging one entire way of life for another.

At least, that is the popular preconception: In the minds of many West-

17

erners, Hungary, Czechoslovakia and Poland have all but disappeared as national entities, absorbed into a homogeneous Marxist monolith. It is true that these countries embody versions of, or attempts at, a socialist state based on the Soviet model. In all three states, political power resides ultimately in the Central Committee of the Communist party. (Although it is known as such only in Czechoslovakia; in Poland, it is called the Polish United Workers' party, and in Hungary, the Socialist Workers' party.) Each one conducts elections to a theoretically independent parliamentary assembly and proclaims itself to be an egalitarian and democratic society. The children of all three countries are educated in the tenets of Marxism-Leninism and are encour-

aged to join socialist youth movements.

In all three countries, the state—in theory, anyway—controls the means of production and supply, owns all industry, sets quotas and prices and gives out jobs. Unemployment is officially unknown. Strikes are banned on the grounds that, since the economy is owned by the state in the name of the proletariat, workers would be striking against themselves—a sophistry that is invoked, not always successfully, to quell dissent. They are all members of the Warsaw Pact, the East's answer to NATO, and the Council for Mutual Economic Assistance (Comecon), a trading consortium of socialist states. And they are all dominated, to varying degrees, by the Soviet Union.

Yet there is another factor of equal

significance linking the countries, and it is that all three have made determined, if unsuccessful, efforts to shake off or transform Soviet Communism, to regain the right to run their own affairs as they see fit. In 1956, three years after the death of Stalin, Hungary staged a national revolution. In 1968, Czechoslovakia tried to introduce a new form of democratic Communism. Two years later, Polish workers rose up and toppled the leadership of First Secretary Władysław Gomułka; then in 1980, a resurgence of working-class militancy led to nationwide strikes, culminating in the formation of Eastern Europe's first independent labor union, Solidarity, in the Baltic shipyard of Gdańsk.

All these attempts at changing an

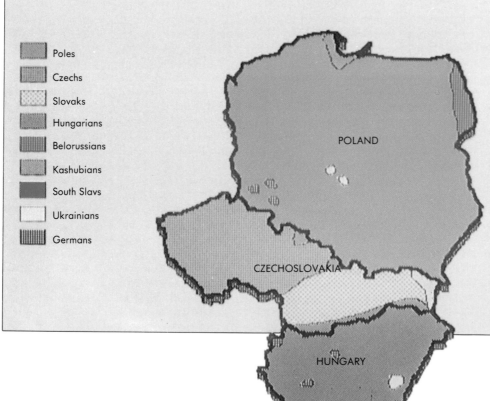

FOOTPRINTS OF SHIFTING POPULATIONS

Poles
Czechs
Slovaks
Hungarians
Belorussians
Kashubians
South Slavs
Ukrainians
Germans

POLAND

CZECHOSLOVAKIA

HUNGARY

In Eastern Europe, centuries of migration and conquest have created a complex ethnic mixture. Most Poles, Czechs and Slovaks descend from Slavs who arrived between 400 and 600 A.D., while the Magyars of Hungary emerged from Asia in the ninth century. Surrounded by these majorities are enclaves of other ethnic groups. The Kashubians of north Poland have retained their identity for centuries, as have Germans whose ancestors came east in the Middle Ages.

But sometimes borders, rather than people, move. When Hungary lost two thirds of its territory after World War I, three million Magyars found themselves living in a foreign country.

alien system were suppressed. In Hungary, more than 2,000 people were killed in fighting with Soviet troops, and a hundred times that number fled into exile. In Czechoslovakia, Warsaw Pact troops invaded Prague, and the country's liberal leader, Alexander Dubček, was toppled from power—to spend the remainder of his career as a minor forestry official. In Poland, after little more than a year of effervescent freedom, martial law was declared and Solidarity suspended.

The upheavals prove, if proof were needed, that national aspirations have not been extinguished. It would be remarkable if this were not the case, for Czechs, Slovaks, Poles and Hungarians have been struggling to affirm their separate identities for more than 1,000 years. They share a Western, Catholic heritage, but they speak different languages, are the issue of different bloodlines and possess tragic, tangled histories that overlapped only sporadically until they found themselves behind the front lines of the Red Army at the end of World War II. "For us, there is no Eastern Europe," asserted the Nobel Prize-winning Czechoslovakian poet Jaroslav Seifert. "It is a collection of countries. . . . You should not see us as a single entity."

Faced with these differences, the Soviet Union has had to allow the leaders of the three countries to tailor Communist doctrine to suit their particular needs and problems. This is the special fascination of Hungary, Czechoslovakia and Poland: three highly individual nations forced to live with a single, imposed political system that each has adapted in its own way. The question of whether that system will survive or whether it will eventually be modified or transformed beyond recognition remains unanswered.

Of the three countries, Hungary seems the least "European," although its capital, Budapest, lies only 170 miles down the Danube from Austria's capital, Vienna. At first the river flows eastward through outliers of the Alps,

At Budapest's Széchényi Baths, the naturally warm outdoor pool teems with bathers seeking the medicinal effects of the numerous minerals in the water. The neobaroque baths, opened in 1881, were built over hot springs known since Roman times.

which form the first third of Hungary's northern border with Czechoslovakia, but then it changes course at the Danube Bend, turning south toward Budapest and cutting the country into two strongly contrasting halves.

On the west bank of the river, in the region called Dunantul or Transdanubia, the landscape is undulating, small-scale and mellow, with ancient forts crowning beech- and oak-covered hills and well-watered valleys that are shared by farms, vineyards and orchards. There, too, lies much of the country's limited mineral resources, notably coal and the bauxite that supplies Hungary's aluminum industry. The eastern half of Hungary is very different. Hungarians call this area the Alföld (Great Plain). It is a flat land where fields stretch away endlessly toward an empty horizon, conveying an impression of spaciousness that belies the country's size—at 35,920 square miles, only a little larger than Ireland.

The Romans began arriving in Transdanubia (called Pannonia in their time) around the first century A.D. and built frontier posts along the west bank of the Danube. By the second century, as many as 20,000 Roman soldiers were deployed along the river between Vienna and Budapest, for the emperors realized that Pannonia's position at the very center of Europe made it either a bulwark against the East or a knife aimed at the West. Time after time, the geography of their land has proved to be the Hungarians' curse, forcing them to ally themselves with whichever power appeared to guarantee their best chance of survival as a political entity. Almost without fail, they have managed to choose the losing side since the 16th century—most recently and regrettably in World War II,

when Hungary sided with Germany in the hope of regaining lost territories.

The Magyars, ancestors of modern Hungarians, were just one of many barbarian peoples that plundered the Carpathian basin and lands to the west after the fall of the Roman Empire. Their closest living relatives are the Finns, the Estonians, and the Vogul and Ostiak tribes of Siberia, who also speak derivatives of the group of languages classified as Finno-Ugric. These are very distant relatives, however, cousins many times removed, whose languages bear little resemblance to modern Hungarian. As a matter of fact, Magyar is an isolated language, and if most Hungarians did not speak some German, communication with foreigners would be virtually impossible.

All Magyars are Hungarians, but not all Hungarians are Magyars. The country's special position at a continental crossroads has produced a melting pot of ethnic groups: Slavs, Turks, Germans, Serbs, Rumanians and even Irish have settled in Hungary. Most are now integrated into the majority nationality. In the mid-1980s, when Hungary's population was 10.7 million—and showing a very slow rate of increase—96.6 percent were classified as Magyar, with the remainder made up of 200,000 Germans, 100,000 Slovaks, 30,000 Southern Slavs and 20,000 Rumanians. More than three fifths of this population were nominally Roman Catholic; there were also Presbyterians, Catholics of the Eastern Rite, Lutherans, Seventh-Day Adventists, Jehovah's Witnesses, Unitarians and fundamentalist Baptists.

Fully 20 percent of all Hungarians live in Budapest. The city is cut in two by the Danube; indeed, Buda and Pest

1

were for many centuries two separate towns facing each other across the river, and they merged only in 1873. Buda, the western half, recalls Hungary's ancient military past: It stands on hills, with forests in the background, its rocky heights crowned by an old citadel, a royal palace and a Gothic coronation church. Pest is the monument to Hungary's coming of age as a modern European state. Most of it was built in the 19th century. Developed on reclaimed marshland on the left, or eastern, bank of the Danube, Pest boasts public buildings and boulevards that emulate Vienna and Paris in their elegance and ornament. They include the university, the stock exchange and the houses of parliament, the largest in Europe when they were completed in 1906, built on the Westminster-Gothic model and topped with a pleasing yet incongruous dome.

With a population of more than two million, Budapest is the largest city not only in Hungary but in Central Europe, exceeding in population such rivals as Prague, Warsaw, Bucharest, Belgrade and Vienna. It dwarfs all other Hungarian towns; the second biggest, Miskolc, an urban-industrial agglomeration 78 miles northeast of Budapest, is only about one tenth its size.

Roads radiate out from Budapest in all directions toward a rim of other small and medium-size towns arranged close to the nation's periphery. The majority of urban dwellers outside Budapest live in Transdanubia—most of them in utilitarian developments of apartment buildings that form residential areas outside well-preserved historic town centers. In Komárom on the Danube, for example, Roman sarcophagi are displayed outside the town council buildings as a reminder that

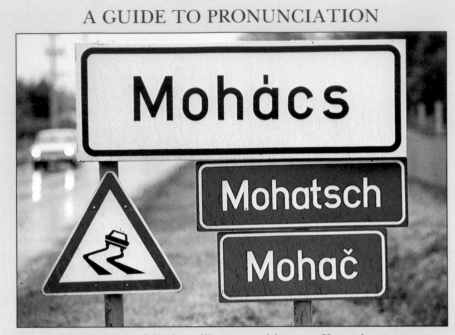

Magyar (top), German and Slavic spellings greet visitors to a Hungarian town.

Three of Eastern Europe's chief languages—Polish, Czech and Slovak—belong to the Western branch of the Slavic family. The fourth, Magyar, or Hungarian—spoken by 13.5 million Eastern Europeans—is unrelated: A member of the Altaic group that includes Korean, its closest relatives are Finnish and Estonian. For many other Eastern Europeans, German is also spoken as a lingua franca, a result of long periods of German influence.

Although written in the familiar characters of the Roman alphabet, all four languages contain perplexing accent marks and spellings. But the pronunciation is relatively consistent, and a few hints can help foreign readers in their attempts at saying the names and common words they encounter. In Czech and Hungarian, the stress always falls on the first syllable of a word; in

Polish it falls on the penultimate.

In Polish, the **dark l** (written ł) sounds like a **w** in English: Lech Wałęsa's name is pronounced **Vawensa:** Vowels marked **ą** or **ę** are spoken with an **n** sound. An accent on a consonant changes it from a simple to a palatalized form: The Polish **s** is pronounced like the **s** in **same** but **ś** as **sh** in **shame; c** as **ts** in **hats** but **ć** as **tch** in **hatch.**

In Czech, the háček also affects the pronunciation of consonants: **ř**—in **Dvořák,** for example—is pronounced as a trilled version of the initial sound in French **gendarme.** Vowels with an accent are long, those without are short.

Hungarian, although it is non-Slavic, has its own method of representing sibilant consonants—for example, **zs** sounds like the **s** in **treasure**—as in the name of Hungarian actress **Zsa Zsa** Gabor.

this was once the northeastern border of the Roman Empire. Midway between Budapest and Vienna is Györ, which has been an important trading center since Roman times and is now best known as a place where the Ikarusz buses commonly seen throughout the Soviet bloc are built.

Sopron, on the Austrian border, was a Roman outpost on the Amber Road, the great trade route linking Byzantium and Vienna. Within its walls, which follow the perimeter of the Roman site, Franz Liszt made his public debut as a pianist at the age of nine. Johann Strauss composed part of his *One Night in Venice* in a Sopron inn, and Joseph Haydn, who was court conductor to Hungary's princely Esterházy family, frequented the town when he was not resident at the Esterházy seat—a huge baroque palace, now a museum, a few miles away. At a time when Hungary was much larger than it is now, the Esterházy family owned one eighth of the country. A member of the family, when told by a 19th-century English nobleman that he had 4,000 sheep, is said to have replied: "In Hungary, sir, I have 4,000 shepherds. I have never counted the sheep."

Szombathely, halfway along the border between Hungary and Austria, claims to be Hungary's oldest town, having been founded by the Roman Emperor Claudius in 42 A.D. It was sacked and largely destroyed in 1241 by a Mongol horde—a fate meted out to most Hungarian towns over the centuries by succeeding waves of invaders. It only returned to its former fortunes in the 18th century, when it was made the seat of a bishopric; now it is a modestly prosperous market town.

The waves of newcomers who have swept over the country in the last 1,000 years have left the most indelible record of their passing on Pécs (pronounced *Pāch)*, which lies amid fertile, hilly country close to the Yugoslavian border. From street to street the character of the town changes: medieval, Turkish, baroque, early-20th-century municipal, or postwar socialist monumental. The most severe cultural collision is in the main square, where there is a 17th-century Turkish mosque on one side and an 11th-century Catholic cathedral on the other. After their victory at the Battle of Mohács, 25 miles to the east, the Turks laid siege to Pécs, which held out for 17 years before finally succumbing in 1543. In the late 20th century, the Turkish mosque still has its *mihrab*, the prayer niche facing Mecca, but symbolically, the Islamic crescent on the dome is surmounted by a Christian cross.

Within the semicircle formed by these western towns, the Transdanubian hills cradle Lake Balaton, which, with a length of 50 miles and an area of 230 square miles, is the largest in Central Europe. It is very shallow, though, averaging about 10 feet deep, which makes it quick to respond to seasonal changes in the weather. Although Hungary has a mild version of a continental climate (a type of climate characterized by hot, dry summers and cold, wet winters), summer temperatures are warm enough to make swimming in the lake a painless proposition as early as May. In winter, the thermometer reading has only to drop slightly below 32° F. for the lake to be frozen by December, when it is used for skating, iceboating and ice fishing.

Summer is the lake's high season: Millions of visitors flock to the resorts and camping grounds that form an almost continuous chain around its shores. Many come for cures at lakeside spas and thermal springs—some of the 500 or so thermal baths in Hungary. The Roman colonists used the springs to heat their houses and planted vineyards on the volcanic soil, giving the ancient province of Pannonia an almost Italianate air that survives in places to this day. But those early settlers had only to travel as far as the Danube and look out across the *puszta*, the prairies of the Great Hungarian Plain, to realize they were a long way from Rome.

Most of the *puszta* is gone, drained

Buyers and sellers mingle at a private car market staged every weekend in Budapest. Only vehicles that are more than three years old may be transferred privately; new cars must be bought through official channels and are subject to heavy taxation.

and plowed in this century to create fields that extend into the distance— searching in vain for the end of the horizon— interrupted occasionally by a road, an isolated farmhouse or a giant open well. But 250,000 acres of *puszta* have been preserved at Hortobágy, a national park some 100 miles east of Budapest, not far from the Rumanian border. It is eerie terrain, where the road winds like a causeway over a sea of waving grass broken by stretches of marsh and alkaline wasteland. There is something sinister and even terrible about this landscape. It is easy to imagine that the mirages that dance in the shimmering air are lines of advancing horsemen. It is difficult to believe that this is Europe.

But if Hungary can look rather alien to Western eyes, its way of life often seems surprisingly similar to that of the West.

Most Hungarians live well. Food markets in Budapest are amply stocked with fresh produce. Red peppers drape stalls like festooned pennants, carp are crammed into fish tanks so tightly that they cannot move a fin in protest; plump geese and legs of pork hang wall to wall in the butchers' shops. Restaurants here are numerous, busy and good. Hungarian cuisine is renowned the world over for *gulyás*, sour cream and paprika—the spice that has become ubiquitous since it was first introduced from the Americas in the 17th century. There are other riches as well: including pike perch from Lake Balaton; quail and venison from the country's game preserves, whose furred and feathered inhabitants are counted as carefully as people (in 1982, they included 26,300 wild boar and 1,529,500 pheasants, of which 851,200 were shot); Tokay from the north, a

golden dessert wine whose praises have been sung by poets for four centuries; and coffee and pastries to equal anything served in Vienna.

However, wages are not particularly high compared with Western countries or even East Germany. But the impression of a prosperous country with what by Soviet standards is a comparatively free economy is no illusion. Since 1956, under the leadership of Party Secretary János Kádár, the nation's business has been increasingly pried loose from the tight grip of the state planners, with widespread decentralization, a limited amount of permitted private enterprise and a stress on profitability rather than on established quotas.

Having shown that it is possible to run a version of the Communist economic system intelligently and relatively efficiently, many Hungarians have reaped benefits. They know that they enjoy the most privileged existence in the Soviet bloc. But they also understand the social implications: Enabling people to satisfy many of their material desires can be a means of diverting them from taking an active interest in politics. "We live in the best barracks in the concentration camp," they say, only half in jest.

A traveler crossing into Czechoslovakia from northeastern Hungary may receive at Eger, 30 miles south of the border, a final reminder that this region was for centuries an outpost of Christendom vulnerably exposed to the Turks. Best known now for its wines, including the robust red called Bull's Blood, Eger was a Turkish provincial capital as late as 1687, and its baroque skyline is punctuated by a solitary minaret, the northernmost in Europe. The sense of being on the fringes

Equipped with a cabin-size tent and a Russian-made car, campers enjoy a trip to the shores of Lake Balaton, Central Europe's largest lake. The average depth of the water is only 10 feet, so Hungary's warm summers quickly bring it to comfortable temperatures for swimming.

Near the village of Tokaj in the northeast of Hungary, a shepherd waters his flock at a traditional sweep well—a pivoting wooden beam with a pail at one end. Hungary has modernized its agriculture but ancient methods still survive in isolated regions.

of the Continent fades, however, as the road winds up and over hills blanketed with hornbeam and oak forests and enters the Slovak Socialist Republic, which, with the Czech Socialist Republic to the west, constitutes the Czechoslovak Socialist Republic.

The Czechoslovak countryside is a fragmented landscape of mountains, fields, forests and sparkling streams, all contained in a relatively small space. Its typical sights seem to be both familiar and yet somehow unreal: brightly painted farmhouses nestled in woodland clearings; Gothic towns with steep, shingled roofs and tall timber-framed gables; municipal halls and rural churches; castles perched on mountain crags. It is the landscape of fairy tales.

The troubled history of Czechoslovakia has more than its share of romance, but few happy endings. The country covers only 49,380 square miles—about the size of New York State—but its borders snake for some 2,175 miles, giving the country common frontiers with Hungary, Austria, West Germany, East Germany, Poland and the Soviet Union. It is not surprising that when Europe has been under stress, the cracks have often appeared first in the Czech Lands. Such was the case in 1419, when the followers of Jan Hus rebelled against the Roman Church; in 1618, when the Czechs revolted against the imperial rule of the Austrian Hapsburgs, triggering the Thirty Years' War; in 1938, when France and Britain sacrificed Czechoslovakia in a vain bid to appease Hitler; in 1948, when the Communists took over in Prague (one of the first moves in the so-called Cold War); and finally in the failed attempt at political liberalization of 1968.

The country has also suffered from internal pressures and divisions, for it is populated by two main ethnic groups—the Czechs of Bohemia and Moravia and the Slovaks of the eastern lands. Bohemia and Moravia occupy the western two thirds of the country, Slovakia the remainder. Out of a total population numbering slightly more than 15

million, about 10 million are Czechs and 4.6 million are Slovaks. In addition, there are 550,000 Hungarians, 45,000 Ukrainians, 65,000 Poles and almost as many Germans.

Although the Czechs and Slovaks speak mutually intelligible languages, derived from a common Slavic root, the two peoples retain their own separate cultural traditions and have their own schools and newspapers. Even the national anthem reflects the split: The first half is a gentle Czech melody and the second half an exuberant Slovak dance. The Czechs are fond of beer; their Slovak compatriots prefer wine. Traditionally, the Slovaks are farmers and foresters, and 20 percent of them still work on the land, though the number is declining. By contrast, the Czechs' skills as precision engineers and manufacturers had put the country among the 10 most highly industrialized countries before the Second World War. Since then, Czech industries have lost their competitiveness with those of Western countries, and East Germany has surpassed Czechoslovakia as an industrial power in the Soviet bloc.

Both Czechs and Slovaks trace their ancestry to Slavs who moved into the area between the fifth and seventh centuries A.D. By the late ninth century, the settlers had come together in a loose confederation known as the Moravian empire, which covered most of modern Czechoslovakia, as well as Hungary and western Poland. But sometime around 900, the Magyars attacked and destroyed the empire, and they seized what is now Slovakia.

For more than 1,000 years, Czechs and Slovaks would follow their own separate paths. The Czechs, after four centuries of autonomy, were absorbed into the empire of their Austrian neighbors. From the 17th century to the beginning of the 20th, they were ruled from Vienna; the lands of their nobility were confiscated, and what was left of the old Czech aristocracy intermarried and became assimilated Austrians.

Slovakia became part of Hungary, and a relatively backward part at that. Although it was not without natural resources, its rich mines and abundant timber would be exploited by outsiders (mainly settlers from Germany) while its indigenous people remained what they had always been: peasants tilling the fields of their landlords. Even after Slovakia was united with the Czech Lands in 1918, it continued to languish as an economic backwater until the postwar socialist government initiated an ambitious program of industrial development. Since that time, the landscape and the local economy have been transformed: Smoke and steam pour out of the massive steel works at Košice; Bratislava, Slovakia's capital and Czechoslovakia's second-largest city, is now the terminal of a 2,500-mile-long pipeline bringing Soviet oil to the region's huge refinery complex.

Slovakia's geography is one reason for a pace of development much slower than that of the neighboring Czech Lands. Except in the south, around the fertile plains of the Danube and its tributaries, Slovakia is hemmed in by hills and mountains, which rise more than 8,700 feet in the High Tatra, the highest section of the Carpathians. South of the Tatra is the Slovenský Kras, the largest karst formation in Europe—310 square miles of limestone hills carved into gorges, chasms and caves, including the Dobšiná Ice Cave, a cavern with a 65-foot-thick floor of ice.

Much of the region is covered by

In Prague's spacious New Town, laid
out in the 19th century, the bright
lights of Wenceslaus Square—actually
a broad avenue—sweep toward the
historic heart of the city. The eques-
trian statue commemorates Prince
Václav (Wenceslaus), who was ruler
of Bohemia in the 10th century.

1

great tracts of fir, spruce, beech, oak and juniper. Czechoslovakia as a whole remains one of the most densely forested countries anywhere in Europe: More than one third of its surface area is wooded, compared with less than 30 percent in Germany and about 27 percent in France.

Cut off from the mainstream of outside influences, Slovakia has preserved many aspects of preindustrial Europe. It still boasts some of the Continent's most varied fauna, including bears, wolves, pine martens, lynxes and chamois. A rich folk culture also survives. On Sundays and local holidays, it is not uncommon to see Slovak men and women wearing elaborate costumes made up of colorful breeches, skirts, aprons and tunics, often decorated with hammered copper, brass and silver. Folk airs are sung to celebrate births, christenings and marriages, and these are backed up by an extraordinary range of accompaniments. Nearly 200 folk instruments have been recorded in Slovakia alone: simple whistles, birdcalls, bagpipes, double bagpipes and dozens of different stringed devices. The government has zealously attempted to foster and preserve these folkways, under the auspices of national programs such as the "Contests of Traditional Crafts."

Czechoslovakia's old industrial heartland, however, is situated in northern Moravia on the far side of the two mountain ranges known as the Little Carpathians and the White Carpathians. Here, the landscape is marked by mining shafts and pitheads and by slag heaps, by ore smelters, foundries and processing plants. What the region lacks in scenic beauty it makes up for in resources of long-standing economic significance: The abundant and easily accessible coal seams, and the once-ample deposits of iron and other metals, put the Czech Lands in the vanguard of European industrial development as early as 1870. But the intensive exploitation that was begun centuries ago has depleted the sources of metal ore.

Not all of Moravia is dominated by soot-blackened chimneys and clangorous factories. The countryside in the south is bucolic, dotted with the fantasies, castles and pleasure gardens of a vanished aristocracy. This is also wine country, where villages lie surrounded by vineyards and where small, family-owned wine cellars are lovingly decorated with folk motifs.

Between Moravia and Bohemia to the west, the boundary is delineated by the Bohemian-Moravian highlands, an important continental watershed, where a distance of 30 feet may be all that separates the source of a river that flows to the North Sea from a spring that flows southward to the Danube and then on to the Black Sea. On a larger scale, these quirks of geography have profoundly affected the whole course of Bohemian history.

The region is boxed in on all sides by mountains, among them the Giant Mountains in the north, the Ore Mountains in the northeast, and the Bohemian highlands in the southwest. Although they are high enough to act as a barrier against the incursions of enemies, these highlands have enough passes and river valleys to allow good communications with other parts of Europe. From the end of the 10th century, an independent Czech state exploited the country's advantages, resisting its neighbors, building towns and castles, constructing roads and opening silver mines, so that by the beginning of the 14th century, Bohemia was one of the most important cultural and commercial centers in Europe.

For a long time, Czech silver was the basis for the Continent's hardest currency. The Czech groat, mined and minted at Kutná Hora, in the center of Bohemia, was accepted by sharp-eyed merchants everywhere from Rome to Stockholm. The Kutná Hora mint was closed in 1726, but much of the medieval town survives, protected by the National Trust for the Preservation of Ancient Monuments.

The trust has an overwhelming task indeed, for Kutná Hora is only one of more than 40 Czechoslovakian towns that have been officially designated for protection. In addition, there are more than 3,000 castles and châteaux, and 40,000 other monuments looked after by the state. These preservation projects range from medieval fishponds, created to breed the carp that are still a major item of Czech cuisine, to 176 mineral springs and spas such as Karlovy Vary and Mariánské Lázně (still more familiar under the old German names of Karlsbad and Marienbad), whose patrons included Beethoven, Chopin, Gogol, Brahms, Bismarck, Dumas, Dvořák and Goethe.

The highest concentration of historical monuments occupies 3.5 square miles of central Prague, the jewel at the heart of Bohemia. The city's beauty has been eulogized since the mid-14th century, when the Holy Roman Emperor Charles IV embarked on a grandiose building program inspired partly by the ambition to make Prague the finest capital in Europe, partly by the need to ease unemployment. The city, which has a population of 1.2 million, rises over seven hills, dominated by the ridge called Hradčany (Castle Hill) crowned

by Prague Castle and the Gothic Cathedral of St. Vitus. The city is divided by the Vltava River, which is still bridged by a span built in Charles' reign. Longevity alone would give the Charles Bridge distinction, but it is also remarkable for its statuary—30 figures of saints placed at intervals along its 1,970-foot length.

Such architectural embellishments abound in Prague. Serpentine cobbled streets lead to baroque churches with bulbous spires and palaces with pink-tiled roofs. Unpromising alleys open onto medieval cloisters or drowsy courtyards. But the details are subordinate to the whole. There is, perhaps, no other city in Europe possessing the same enchantment—enchantment that comes from the perfect blending of nature and human achievement.

The Prague cityscape also expresses another variety of synthesis: the meeting of the indigenous Bohemian culture with that of the German-speaking peoples who have exerted political and intellectual influences on the city for at least 600 years. Medieval Bohemia's booming economy attracted perspicacious German merchants who settled and prospered, and until the present century, Prague remained as much a German city as a Czech one.

Like the Czechs and the Slovaks, the Poles have had to fight to retain or recover their national identity after many centuries of outside domination. Throughout its thousand-year history, Poland has been the prey of its expansionist neighbors.

A clue to Poland's turbulent past can be found in its name, which derives from *pole*, the local word for "field." Much of the country lies astride the Northern European Plain, a swath of

Rising more than 8,000 feet, the snow-covered peaks of the High Tatra sparkle above frozen fields near the village of Štrba in the heartland of Slovakia. Štrba, on the shores of a glacier lake, is a popular ski resort and year-round vacation spot.

lowland that stretches across Europe from northern France to the Urals. Lacking any major natural barriers to east and west, exposed to invasion from Germany or Russia, Poland has been engaged from its inception in a struggle to establish firm borders. During this struggle, the country has shifted back and forth across the map of Europe, expanding and contracting according to the fortunes of its armies. Between 1795 and 1914, it even disappeared altogether as an independent nation.

Ironically, after all the vicissitudes of history, modern Poland occupies virtually the same territory that it did under its first ruler, Mieszko I, leader of a Slavonic tribe called the Polanie. At 120,734 square miles, it is the seventh-largest country in Europe—about the size of the United Kingdom and the Irish Republic combined.

Outside the flat central plain, Poland boasts scenery as varied and spectacular as any in Europe. In the south are the Tatra and Sudeten mountains and other lesser, but equally beautiful, ranges—including the Pieniny, which is pierced by a magnificent 5.6-mile-long river gorge whose sides tower as much as 985 feet above the Dunajec River. In the northeast, on the Soviet border, is the Białowieża Forest, the last tract of primeval woodland in Europe—480 square miles of fir, pine, oak, hornbeam, lime, ash and other species, many of them well over 130 feet tall and more than 500 years old. Its greatest claim to fame, however, is that the forest shelters the only remaining herd of European bison, animals otherwise extinct in the wild.

In the north are the lake districts of Mazuria and Pomerania. The lakes, surrounded by glacial debris deposited during the last Ice Age, number more

31

1

than 9,000 and range from tiny woodland pools to large bodies of water such as Mamry and Śniardwy, which have areas of more than 40 square miles apiece. To summertime visitors, this maze of forests and waterways may seem like an idyll rediscovered: Sunlight plays on leaves and water; elk, deer and beaver may be surprised at the water's edge; and eagles on huge square wings glide over rafts of waterfowl. But the same scene can seem unbearably melancholy in the bitter-cold winters, when the forests lie rigid and soundless and mists hang on the ponds, stained by a blood red sun that barely rises above the trees. It is easy then to understand why pagan rites persisted in this region long after the rest of Poland had embraced Christianity.

Poland also has a 310-mile Baltic coastline—a gently rolling coastal plain fringed with extensive sandy beaches, shifting dunes and rocky islets, punctuated by numerous resorts and fishing villages. The coast even includes a "desert"—12 square miles of shifting sands in the village of Łeba, so like the deserts of North Africa that Rommel used it to train troops of the Afrika Korps during the German occupation in World War II.

Farther south, in the central plain, lie countless small, somnolent country towns, each one much like every other. A visitor, driving into one of these communities along dusty, ill-paved streets, is likely to be trapped behind vehicles moving at a gentler, more bucolic pace than his own: an antique, shuddering tractor, belching diesel exhaust, or perhaps a long, horse-drawn, lantern-lit farm cart. Roads lined with one-story houses, their color-washed plaster fronts peeling gently, and a few small, sparsely stocked or shuttered shops, will lead to a central square dominated, inevitably, by an imposing Roman Catholic church.

Leaving town, the streets peter out, with surprising suddenness, into quiet lanes where geese stride through the mud and storks nest in cottage chimneys. On the outskirts there will be a

cemetery, its ranked white crosses decorated with flowers and photographs of the dead. And often, just where settlement gives way to field and forest, a small road sign points the way to a different sort of memorial: one of the many mass graves of World War II victims who were marched off by the invaders to an old quarry or a pine forest, shot and buried where they fell.

The war left a deep wound in Polish society that has yet to heal. In 1939, the country's population was 35 million. Forty-five years later, it was about 37 million, despite a tremendous postwar baby boom that has made young people between the ages of 20 and 29 the largest age group in the country.

That the baby boom has not increased the population by much is due partly to territorial changes at the end of the war. Poland lost nearly 50 percent of its former territory—mainly in the east—to the Soviet Union, while it gained German provinces in the west. In this way, the country's borders were effectively moved approximately 125 miles farther west.

This geographical shift was accompanied by social and economic upheavals. The new Poland possesses quite different resources from the old, having exchanged the rural districts of the east—which have become part of the U.S.S.R.—for the industrial and seaboard districts of the former German lands. And it possesses a different society, more ethnically homogeneous in some ways, for the Jewish, German and Ukrainian communities that formed more than a quarter of the prewar population are now largely gone, either murdered or banished.

The most terrible trauma of the war, of course, was its human cost. More

than six million Poles were killed during the conflict—a casualty rate of 18 percent, compared with 0.2 percent in the United States, less than 1 percent in Great Britain, 7.4 percent in Germany and 11.2 percent in the Soviet Union. Less than 100,000 of these deaths were incurred in the 35 days that it took the German *Blitzkrieg* to roll over Poland; the rest, including most of Poland's three million Jews, died in brave but futile uprisings, were murdered in savage German reprisals or perished in the concentration camps.

No city in the world, with the exception of Hiroshima, suffered as dreadfully as the Polish capital, Warsaw. In the course of the war, 800,000 Poles died there—200,000 of them in the nine-week Warsaw uprising against the Nazi occupying forces in 1944. While the revolt ran its tragic course, Soviet troops that had reached the outskirts of the city halted in their advance, doing nothing to end the slaughter.

By the time the Red Army did enter the capital in January of 1945, they found it in ruins. Before the Germans retreated, orders had been given by

their Supreme Commander, Adolf Hitler himself, for the destruction of the entire city. "Annihilation corps" units were sent in to remove all valuables that could be plundered from the buildings. Then, armed with flamethrowers and dynamite, they burned and blew up literally everything, street by street. They tore up the city's trolley tracks and telephone cables, destroyed its electric-power and sewage systems and even uprooted its trees.

The Soviet Army belatedly moved in to put an end to the insanity. But by that time, nearly 90 percent of Warsaw had been razed or reduced to roofless, floorless shells. All told, more than 11,000 buildings were totally destroyed and an additional 14,000 were severely damaged. Of the city's 957 historic buildings, 782 lay in ruins, and more than 90 percent of its factories had been wiped out.

Today it is difficult to imagine the devastation that confronted the Poles. Faced with the task of clearing 20 million tons of rubble, in which 100,000 German mines had been hidden, the postwar authorities could have been

33

forgiven for simply abandoning Warsaw and transferring the capital elsewhere. Instead, within two weeks of the liberation, the Polish Council of Ministers declared that the city would be rebuilt. Priority was given to the reconstruction of the Old Town, an enclave of narrow houses, little winding streets and numerous churches clustered around a cobblestone market place. Working from the original plan, which had been hidden from the Germans, from detailed views painted by the 18th-century artist Bernardo Bellotto, the nephew of Canaletto, and from prints and old photographs in private collections, Polish architects, historians, builders and masons, assisted by volunteers and German prisoners of war doing forced labor, put the whole town together again.

The best vantage point from which to admire the rebuilt city, as its citizens will tell you, is from the top of the 37-story Palace of Culture and Science. Why? Because it is the only spot in Warsaw from which you can avoid looking at the Palace of Culture and Science—a skyscraper in jarring Soviet "wedding-cake" style. In fact, the 768-foot pinnacle does provide a breathtaking vista of a city that has been restored to its prewar size and 1.6 million population. Its industries have also been refurbished, and to their number have been added new ones, including a large steelworks to the north of the city and an automobile factory in Praga, the traditionally working-class area east of the Vistula River. Beyond the picturesque narrow streets of the Old Town, however, Warsaw is spacious, with long avenues and numerous parks surrounding large apartment buildings. Much of the residential architecture is utilitarian and undistinguished, but as a symbol of re-

surgence, rising phoenix-like from the ashes of World War II, the city as a whole is a triumph.

Few Polish towns emerged from the war unscathed, and in most cities, the damage was on a large scale. Poznań, an important trading center midway between Warsaw and Berlin, lost 50 percent of its prewar structures, while 70 percent of the buildings disappeared in Wrocław, a German town in the southwest that was repopulated after the war largely by settlers coming in from Poland's former eastern provinces.

Only Kraków in the south, the Polish capital until the beginning of the 17th century, escaped destruction: The German occupying forces were outflanked by the Red Army and forced to flee the city before they could blow it up. This was a marvelous deliverance, for Kraków is home to one of Europe's finest assemblages of medieval and Renaissance architecture.

The city is also a repository of Poland's history. Priceless national treasures are kept in the castle that crowns the Wawel, a rocky limestone outcrop on the banks of the Vistula. They include the sword used in the coronation of Polish kings since 1320 and a collection of four-room Turkish tents captured at the siege of Vienna in 1683, when a charge led by the Polish King Jan Sobieski broke the Ottoman ranks and forced a retreat, permanently halting the Turks' advance into Europe. In the cathedral next to the castle, the former see of Pope John Paul II, Sobieski lies buried alongside other national heroes, including Tadeusz Kościuszko, who distinguished himself in the American Revolution and later returned to Poland to lead an abortive but valiant uprising.

Below the Wawel, in Kraków's market square, reputedly the biggest and most splendid market place in Europe, four trumpet calls, each ending on a sudden high note, signal each hour—immortalizing the memory of a watchman whose trumpeted warning of the approach of a Tatar army in 1241 was abruptly halted by an enemy arrow. The same haunting call is broadcast at noon each day on Polish radio.

The luster of so many of Poland's cities may come as a surprise to visitors whose picture of the country has been formed by television news footage of the 1980s showing scenes of labor unrest in grimly industrial settings. A city that conforms more closely to this uglier image is Katowice, the capital of Silesia, Poland's coal-rich southern province. All around the town, chimney stacks belch smoke into the sky and untidy slag heaps scar the landscape. Here, in the winter of 1981, miners occupied the Piast coal mine—the last group to hold out against the imposition of martial law and the accompanying suppression of the independent labor union Solidarity.

What ended at Katowice had begun during the previous summer in the Baltic port of Gdańsk. Strikes staged there in protest against a rash of food price increases ultimately led to the formation of a national movement that was joined by 90 percent of the Polish work force. Officially, spokesmen for Solidarity said that the union had been formed to protect the interests of the workers in the face of a disastrous economic situation. Poland was on the verge of bankruptcy, with international debts higher than those of the Soviet Union itself. The Polish złoty was virtually worthless; even privileged sections of the work force such as the Ka-

towice miners, who earned three times the national average wage, could find few goods to buy with their money.

In a country with more than one fifth of its surface covered by forests, matches were virtually unobtainable. In a country that is the fourth-largest exporter of coal in the world, fuel for domestic consumption was in such short supply that power cuts were a common occurrence. In a country where 30 percent of the population work on the land, meat and butter were strictly rationed, as were alcohol, tobacco, soap, gasoline, shoes and underwear. All these items were available on the black market. But for the ordinary worker, who was almost always unable

to pay several times the official rate for under-the-counter goods, the situation became intolerable.

Solidarity was not merely a labor union; it was a mass movement for political reform that threatened the least effective party leadership in Eastern Europe. For a few months, before being outlawed by the state, it virtually was Poland, embodying the unique blend of nationalism and Catholicism central to the Polish sense of identity. Inevitably, an organization that commanded more allegiance than the government did could not be tolerated for long. In December of 1981, control of the country was taken by General Jaruzelski and a Military Council for Na-

tional Salvation. Martial law was imposed and Solidarity banned.

Despite widespread sympathy—and truck loads of emergency supplies—from the West, the Poles suffered from a sense of isolation. It was not a new sensation. An age-old cry of the Polish intelligentsia, expressing their feeling of living on the periphery of Europe, has been: "God is too high above, and France too far away." With its political ties in one direction and its spiritual and intellectual affiliations in the other, Poland remains the ideological battleground of Eastern Europe—the place where the rival cultures and philosophies of East and West confront each other in their most acute form. □

Around the village of Bukowina in the Tatra foothills, tidy hayfields reflect the pattern of Polish land use: Privately owned holdings average only

12.4 acres. Poland's private farmers, who have resisted collectivization, produce almost 77 percent of the agricultural output.

HISTORIES WRITTEN IN BLOOD

Malbork Castle, the largest Gothic fortress in Europe, guards Poland's Nogat River southeast of present-day Gdańsk. Constructed between the 13th and 15th centuries as headquarters for the empire-building Teutonic Knights, the castle stands as a brooding reminder of foreign domination.

An almost-endless succession of invading armies has roared across the lands between the Danube River and the cold gray waters of the Baltic Sea:

the siege continues for so long a time the
*   enemies have to change*
they have nothing in common but the desire
*   to annihilate us*
when some hordes depart others immediately
*   appear*
Goths, Tatars, Swedes imperial
*   legions. . . .*

In his *Report from a Town under Siege,* written in 1982, Poland's Herbert Zbignlew is speaking of his homeland; but no Hungarian, Slovak or Czech could fail to empathize. For centuries, these nations have led their political lives under stress, engaged in a perpetual struggle to preserve their linguistic autonomy and cultural cohesion from more powerful neighbors. All have known long periods of alien rule or foreign occupation—times of being held as pawns by larger powers. Their near neighbors—notably the Turks to the south, the Russians to the east and the Germans to the west—have been among the more voracious empire builders, all too ready to gobble up the weaker nations in their paths.

The fact that Poland, Hungary and Czechoslovakia exist is a measure of the tenacity with which they have defended their national identities. Not one of these three countries, however, has the same boundaries today that it had 50 or 100 years ago; indeed, the state of Czechoslovakia is a 20th-century creation entirely, one that unites two Slavic peoples who sprang from the same ancient stock.

The region's prehistory begins at the very dawn of European civilization. Archeologists have found traces of important settlements dating from the 10th and 12th millennia B.C. The Scythians were one of the earliest identifiable peoples, nomads remembered as the finest goldsmiths the world has ever known. The Celts, who moved down the Danube during the fourth century B.C. were another early group of inhabitants; they brought with them such innovations as the potter's wheel and the minting of coins.

The Romans followed early in the second century A.D., although they never ventured far beyond the banks of the Danube, which for a time constituted the eastern boundary of the Roman Empire. By then, much of the region had been settled by tribes whose homelands were probably farther to the east. Little is known about them except that they spoke Slavic languages—the rootstocks of modern Russian, Polish, Czech, Slovak, Serbo-Croatian and Bulgarian—and lived in loosely connected communities as hunters, herders, or tillers of the soil.

Between the fourth and seventh centuries, during the great migrations of Asian and European populations after

A 15th-century illustration shows Czech religious reformer Jan Hus on his way to the stake, condemned for heresy. Unlike most clerics, Hus preached in the vernacular, as well as in Latin, to reach a wider public. His attacks on corruption in the Church found a sympathetic audience.

the decline of the Roman empire, wave after wave of nomadic peoples poured into the region, mainly from the east and northeast. Invading Huns established a short-lived empire, and another Eastern people, the Avars, ruled what is now Hungary for some 200 years. Slavic tribes, pressing on the heels of Teutonic immigrants, gradually occupied almost all the land as far west as the Elbe River.

In Charlemagne's time, the tide flowed the other way. The Saxons from west of the Elbe took over much of the Slav-occupied lake district west of the Vistula River, starting the proverbial German *Drang nach Osten* (Drive to the East) that was to play a vital role in the next 1,000 years of European history. To meet the Saxon threat, some of the Slavic tribes united to form the nucleus of the state—a "kingdom" mentioned briefly in one of the old chronicles. Farther to the south, the equally shadowy Slav empire of Moravia, which had been established earlier in the ninth century, quickly disintegrated when, in 896, the plains of Hungary were overrun by the Magyars. The Magyars were seven allied tribes of nomadic horsemen from homelands west of the Volga. They were led by Prince Árpád, the founder of a dynasty that would remain in power for 300 years.

The Magyars, known as the On-Ogurs, or "people of the ten arrows," seemed to have been born on horseback. Trained from infancy as riders, archers and javelin throwers, they attacked in successive waves that terrorized the static rows of armed peasants who took the field against them. They ravaged the Danube and Elbe valleys and plundered Germany from Bavaria to Saxony; some of the On-Ogurs' raids reached into France. The Germans'

King Henry I found that the only effective defense was to organize a hard-riding cavalry of his own. As resistance stiffened, the On-Ogurs gave up murderous incursions and settled on their On-Ogurian (hence, Hungarian) plain as farmers and stock breeders. But they never lost their ability to wage war on horseback: Even in the late 20th century, the ancient Magyar art of fencing with the cavalry saber is faithfully practiced as a national sport.

Perhaps the most important step in the transformation of the warlike On-Ogurs into peaceful Hungarians was their conversion to Christianity around 1000 A.D., which gave them not only a priestly class that could read and write but a new faith, the universal religion of civilized Europe. At first, the Magyar rulers considered adopting Greek Orthodoxy, the form of Christianity practiced in Byzantium; but that Eastern empire was an uncomfortably ambitious neighbor. As a counterweight to its influence—for even then the balance of power played a decisive role in political calculations—Géza of Hungary arranged for Roman Catholic missionaries from Germany to baptize him and his entire family.

In 1001, Pope Sylvester II recognized the Magyar state by endowing Géza's successor, Stephen, with a royal crown. Under Stephen I—later to be canonized Saint Stephen—the whole of the country was brought into the Roman Catholic fold. And it is that royal diadem that now is displayed in the Hungarian National Museum at Budapest as the most precious symbol of Hungarian sovereignty.

The Slavic peoples of Poland, Bohemia and Moravia were converted to Christianity about the same time, also under Roman Catholic tutelage and under pressure from neighboring German princes intent on eliminating the threat of paganism from their borders. By becoming Christian, a Slavic monarch could hope to find a place in the increasingly influential Holy Roman Empire of the German nation—a union of states and princes headed by an emperor who received his crown from the pope and derived his title from the Caesars.

In 1000, the Holy Roman Emperor Otto III recognized the Christian warrior-monarch Bolesław the Brave as king of Poland, and Bolesław's domain soon extended from the Baltic to the Carpathians and from the Elbe as far as the Bug River.

Yet this immense kingdom was too weak to withstand the pressures pulling it apart: Local princelings battled one another, jockeying for power, more interested in promoting their separate regional interests than in preserving the kingdom as a whole. Bolesław's successors were forced to partition Poland into four—and later eight—principalities; the two centuries that followed have become known as the Period of Fragmentation. Not until 1320 was a Polish prince again crowned king of a united Poland.

Meanwhile, the whole of Eastern Europe had been devastated by a new and terrifying force from central Asia, the Tatars of the "Golden Horde." Led by the Mongol chieftain Batu, a grandson of Genghis Khan, the Tatars swept through Russia into southern and central Poland; reduced Kraków and other cities to ashes; routed the confederated princes of Silesia; and then invaded Hungary, where Batu defeated King Béla IV on the banks of the Sajó. At last, they turned back to Russia, where they established a khanate that remained a great power for several hundred years. The duchies of northern Russia were subjugated to the grand khan until the end of the 14th century, when they liberated themselves and joined under the rule of the duke—later the tsar—of Muscovy. In the Crimean Peninsula, the Tatars held sway until the 1700s.

To repopulate the regions ravaged by the Tatars, the rulers of Poland invited foreign settlers into their lands—among them Dutch, Czechs, Flemings and Walloons, but above all Germans, who were promised special privileges and better living conditions than they had enjoyed at home. The so-called German colonization brought tens of thousands of Germans into the walled cities of western Poland and later into the eastern provinces and Lithuania, where they played a major role in rebuilding ruined towns and establishing new ones. Thousands of German Jews, as well as Jewish immigrants from Kiev and southern Russia, settled in Poland. Sometimes they lived in villages of their own; but more often they moved to the cities, where with the Germans and Armenians, they formed a flourishing middle class of merchants and artisans. This middle class gave agricultural Poland a new market economy, with trade routes reaching from Asia to France and the British Isles.

Developments in the kingdom of Bohemia followed much the same pattern. The 13th-century Czech ruler Přemysl Otakar II—known as "the man of gold" on account of his wealth and as "the man of iron" in recognition of his military prowess—encouraged immigration by German settlers in the hope that prosperous German townsmen would strengthen his hand against

2

the increasing power of the Bohemian nobles. The German settlers received special privileges to help them succeed as merchants and artisans—but the Germans' favored status created discord between them and the Czechs. The conflict was exacerbated by the fact that the Germans held the wealthier and more powerful positions in the Catholic Church, while the lower, poorly paid offices went to the Czech clergy.

Otakar's grandson, Václav III—at 17 the last king of the native Czech Přemyslid dynasty—was murdered by unknown assassins in 1306. To succeed him, the Bohemian nobles elected John of Luxembourg, husband of a Přemyslid princess, to the throne. Though John himself neglected his kingdom, he founded a dynasty that ruled Bohemia for more than 130 years. His son, Charles I—styled Charles IV when wearing his other crown as Holy Roman Emperor—proved to be one of the great rulers of Bohemia. His memory is particularly revered in Prague, a city he endowed with one of the first universities in Europe and with a Nové Město, or New Town, which unlike the German populated Old City, was to be inhabited mainly by Czechs.

The smoldering resentment between the richer Germans and the more numerous Czechs finally came to a head early in the 15th century, when the Czech cleric Jan Hus, one of the university's early rectors, attempted to reform the Church in Bohemia. Like the English reformer John Wycliffe (and like Martin Luther a century later), Hus protested against the Church's sale of indulgences and other worldly abuses, proclaiming, "In the things that pertain to salvation, God is to be obeyed rather than man." Hus's doctrine had a Bohemian-nationalist bias that made him a hero to the Czech lower gentry and the common people but an anathema to the Germans, who saw him as a threat to the privileged position that they enjoyed in church and state.

When the ruler of Germany, Sigismund, convened the Council of Constance in 1414, Hus received a royal safe-conduct and was called to appear before the council to defend his position. Once in Constance, however, he was charged with heresy, found guilty and burned at the stake. His execution aroused indignation throughout Bohemia and strengthened the intransigence of his followers, the Hussites. In Prague, a Hussite procession was stoned from the town hall, apparently by the burgomaster and several of his aides. The incensed marchers stormed the building and threw their assailants out the windows.

Václav IV, Charles I's son, was seized with a fatal attack of apoplexy when he heard of the incident, known to history as the First Defenestration of Prague (others followed in later centuries). Attempts to reach a compromise between Catholic traditionalists and the would-be reformers failed. The Hussites rose in revolt and waged open warfare against the papist armies hastily assembled by Sigismund, who as Václav's half brother had succeeded to the Bohemian throne on the king's death. The insurgents, who referred to themselves as God's Warriors, marched into battle singing hymns and carrying homemade weapons, striking fear into the hearts of the mercenaries who opposed them. Sigismund was not able to capture Prague. His forces were defeated in 1420 and again in 1422.

During the decade that followed, the Hussites were so successful that they became bolder and more ambitious and repeatedly invaded Hungary and the German states. But they divided into two warring factions themselves: The more aristocratic wing raised an "army of the nobles," while the Taborites, the populist party, mustered an "army of the towns." When the two armies met on the battlefield of Lipany on the 30th of May, 1434, the Taborites were virtually annihilated.

In the aftermath, the Czech nobles worked out a compromise with the crown that gave them limited religious freedom; the Czech peasants were reduced to the status of serfs, losing all their rights as citizens. When the Bohemian throne fell vacant in 1457, a Hussite nobleman, George of Poděbrady, was unanimously elected king of the Estates of Bohemia; but his efforts to arrange a lasting peace with the pope proved ineffectual. The ensuing civil war ended only with Poděbrady's death in 1471: In Czech history he has occupied a special place as the last king who actually came from Bohemia and the only one who was not a Roman Catholic.

While the Czechs were struggling to preserve the identity of what has been described as "a small Slav promontory in a German sea," the Hungarians were locked in a life-and-death conflict with the expanding Turkish Empire. The Ottoman Turks, who had come from the East in the 14th century, conquered Constantinople and the Balkans and were soon knocking at the gates of Hungary. The Árpád dynasty had exhausted its energies after 300 years of rule, and the country was on the verge of anarchy. Fortunately, Hungary was governed for much of the 14th century by two highly capable kings of the House of Anjou, Charles I and Louis I, who restored law and order to a country swarming with brigands and robber barons.

Louis, called "the Great," added the crown of Poland to that of Hungary in 1370. Though sharing a monarch, the principalities remained separate kingdoms within a domain that stretched from the Baltic to the Danube and from the Adriatic to the Dnieper. Sigismund, who was later to play such an ineffectual role in Bohemian affairs, was crowned king of Hungary in 1387, after marrying the daughter of Louis the Great. His attempt to roll back the Turkish advance ended in crushing defeat for the Christian army at Nicopolis (now Nicopol, Bulgaria) in 1396. Even so, Sigismund had the foresight to reinforce the defenses of the small fort that was eventually to become the mighty citadel of Belgrade, at the strategic junction of the Danube and the Sava rivers in present-day Yugoslavia. It proved strong enough to repel all Turkish attacks for the next 100 years.

Sigismund's abiding need for funds to conduct his campaigns forced him to convoke a legislative council of Magyar nobles who could be called on to provide taxes for his war chest. Hence, for the first time, Hungary had something like an assembly of notables to advise the king. Great landowners were also obliged to furnish large numbers of archers and horsemen for the wars against the Turks. Yet the best youths of Magyar chivalry, led by the young

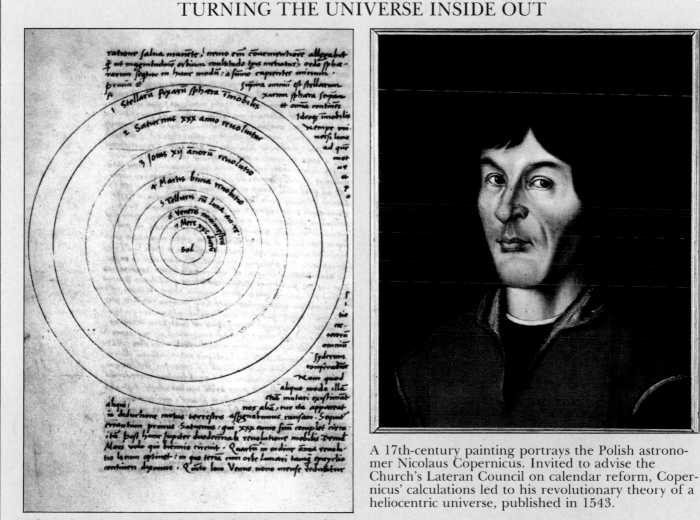

TURNING THE UNIVERSE INSIDE OUT

A Copernican chart correctly places the planets in a solar orbit.

A 17th-century painting portrays the Polish astronomer Nicolaus Copernicus. Invited to advise the Church's Lateran Council on calendar reform, Copernicus' calculations led to his revolutionary theory of a heliocentric universe, published in 1543.

2

Polish king, Władysław III (who was crowned king of Hungary in 1440) were annihilated by the Turks at Varna in Bulgaria while on yet another ill-starred crusade.

Władysław's successor came, for a change, from a noble Hungarian family, the Hunyadi: On January 24, 1458, some 40,000 Hungarian nobles assembled on the frozen ice of the Danube to elect as king of Hungary Mátyás Hunyadi. He went on to reign for more than 30 years with enormous military and political éclat. In the Hungarian view of history, Mátyás Corvinus—so named because of the raven (Latin *corvus*) in his coat of arms—ranks as the greatest man of his day and as one of the greatest monarchs of the Renaissance. To establish his right to the throne, he conducted several swift campaigns against rival claimants—Casimir IV of Poland and German Emperor Frederick III. Of equal importance, he taught the Turks not to trespass on Hungarian territory: He and his horsemen destroyed a huge Ottoman army returning from a plundering expedition in Transylvania.

Yet Mátyás was also an illustrious statesman, orator, legislator, and administrator; a generous and unvindictive ruler; a patron of poets and artists; a voracious reader, as well as a collector of books and works of art. His subjects called him Mátyás the Just. Still, in these violent times the humanity of a Renaissance prince had always to be balanced against the military skills of a leader of armies. It was Mátyás who created the famous Hungarian light cavalry called the Hussars. Wearing wolfskins over the left shoulder as a symbol of their prowess and defiance, they were soon feared throughout Europe as, in the words of a contemporary

THE TRUE TALE OF A VAMPIRE COUNTESS

The sadistic exploits of Elizabeth Báthory, known as the Blood Countess, inspired parts of Bram Stoker's novel *Dracula*.

Born in 1560, Elizabeth was the daughter of an aristocratic Hungarian family favored with wealth and tainted with madness. They were kin by marriage to the Draculas, who were, in fact, a historic Eastern European clan; the dragon eating its tail *(below)* appears in the crests of both houses. At 15, Elizabeth married Ferenc Nádasdy, a soldier whose long campaigns left his bride very much alone.

Elizabeth amused herself by torturing her serving maids. She burned them with hot irons, cut off their fingers, even bit them in her rage. After her husband's death in 1604, she began murdering girls outright, by beating, freezing or starving them. Her lackeys lured victims to the castle to ever more ingenious deaths. According to legend, Elizabeth bathed in the maidens' blood to smooth her skin.

In 1610, rumors of Elizabeth's deeds reached the king of Hungary, Matthias. At the subsequent trial of Elizabeth's accomplices, the number of victims was estimated at 650. The countess was never tried. Condemned to life imprisonment by the king, she was walled up in a room of her castle, where she died in 1614.

Below a portrait of Elizabeth Báthory the ruins of her home, 13th-century Castle Čachtice, loom over the Czech landscape. Its cellars served as the countess's torture chamber.

2

chronicler, "an exceedingly ravenous and cruell kynde of men." But they kept the Turks at bay.

Poland, in the meantime, enjoyed a resurgence of prosperity after the Tatar threat receded. The newly independent Polish cities, with their charters of rights and privileges, became the favorite meeting places where merchants from East and West bought and sold furs, silks and spices, as well as the more prosaic goods that traveled along northern trade routes now that the Mediterranean and surrounding area had become a battleground between Islam and Christianity.

Encircled by massive walls and turreted fortifications, the great market towns had their own municipal councils, their merchants' and artisans' guilds, their lofty Gothic cathedrals and parish churches, and their broad squares flanked by imposing town halls. Kraków, situated on the Vistula at the point where the river becomes navigable, was important not only for trade and the transshipment of merchandise but as a center of medieval learning, the seat of a university nearly as old as that of Prague. It attracted scholars from every country in Europe, and the library was renowned for its treasures. The students and professors of Kraków played a notable role during the days of the New Learning that ushered in a

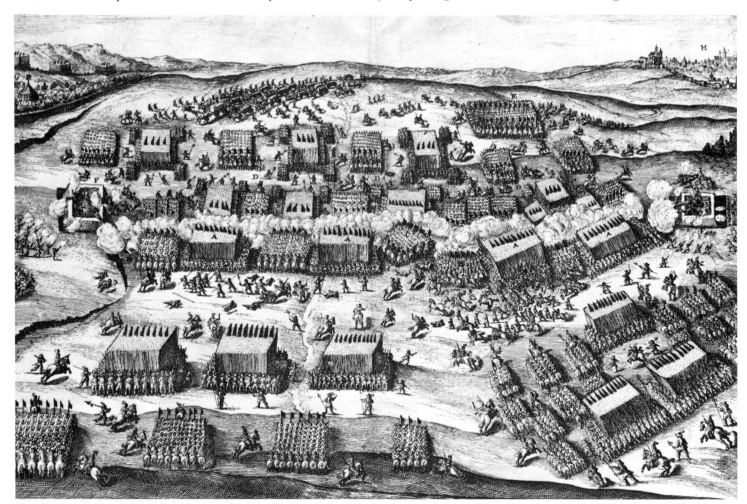

In a 17th-century engraving by Wenceslaus Hollar, Protestant Czech rebels challenge the forces of their Catholic Hapsburg king at the Battle of the White Mountain in 1620. The rebels' defeat brought suppression of their language and religion, prompting widespread emigration.

fresh scientific and philosophical perception of the world.

The power and importance of the Polish crown had been vastly increased toward the end of the 14th century, when young Polish Queen Jadwiga married Jagiełło, Grand Duke of neighboring Lithuania, and thus brought about the union of the two states under a single crown. The Lithuanians and their duke were converted from paganism to Christianity at the same time—a mass baptism that robbed the missionaries, known as the Knights of the Teutonic Order, of their pretext for invading the grand duchy.

Until then, this powerful order of German knights had been allowed to occupy vast parts of the region so that they could fulfill their avowed mission of bringing Christianity to the heathen. In fact, they acted as a curious conglomerate of religious, military and economic interests, extending German rule deep into Slavic territory. Gradually, they moved their bases eastward without relinquishing the towns and cities they already held, notably Danzig (present-day Gdańsk), Königsberg, Elbing, Marienburg and Thorn.

At the height of their power, the Teutonic Knights controlled all of the territory between the Vistula River and the Gulf of Finland. Commanderies were established everywhere to hold the conquered Slavs and Balts in subjugation; churches and monasteries were given the task of instructing the former pagans in the Christian religion. Prussia alone contained 55 large fortified cities and towns in which only German was to be spoken, and Slavic languages were banned in an attempt to prevent people from hatching conspiracies or backsliding into idolatry. At the same time, the knights deliberately excluded the Slavs from the ports along the Baltic and negotiated commercial treaties with other maritime nations as though they were independent sovereigns.

Not surprisingly, the kings of Poland began to see the Teutonic Knights as trespassers and dangerous rivals. In 1410, Jagiełło led an army of Poles and Lithuanians—reinforced by Russians and Tatars—against the Teutonic Knights, and inflicted a crushing defeat on their armies at the Battle of Grünwald. Grand Master Ulrich von Jungingen was slain, as were hundreds of knights and thousands of soldiers. Nevertheless, the struggle to evict the knights from their strongholds continued until the 1460s, when the most prominent king of the Jagiellonian dynasty, Casimir IV, finally expelled the order from the western part of its domains and compelled the knights to acknowledge him as their sovereign in eastern Prussia.

Yet even as the threat from the Teutonic Knights subsided, new problems arose in the East, where Polish ambitions clashed with the growing power of the tsars of Muscovy. At issue was the control of the borderlands. Hitherto populated by nomads, these extensive plains and lowlands were now being opened to settlement; they were to become a centuries-long subject of conflict between Poles and Russians—and between the Greek Orthodox and Roman Catholic churches. For the time being, the Poles extended their influence southward into the Ukraine, stretching from Kiev to the Black Sea. The Ukraine was controlled by a band of hardy fighters formed by fugitive serfs who had escaped into the wilderness and who became known as Kazaki (a Tatar word for "plunderers"), or Cossacks. They accepted Polish sovereignty, at the same time retaining a high degree of autonomy.

The religious upheavals that accompanied the Protestant Reformation in Germany also sent violent tremors through Poland; but in the end, its people remained firmly in the Catholic camp. Greater troubles ensued after the death of the last of the Jagiellonian kings in the 1570s. The country's quarrelsome nobles, who took a grim pride in their everlasting disagreements, could find no suitable Polish successor and insisted on placing a sequence of foreigners on the throne. Their first choice, Henry of Valois, ruled for only 13 months. The second, iron-fisted Stephen Bátory, a prince of Transylvania, had a longer and more notable career. In his 11 years as king of Poland, he quelled an uprising in Danzig, "the pearl of the Baltic," and scored a series of military and diplomatic victories over a formidable array of opponents: Tsar Ivan the Terrible of Muscovy, the sultan of the Ottoman Empire and Hapsburg rulers of the Holy Roman Empire.

In Hungary, however, the overwhelming might of the Turkish army had finally shattered the nation's defenses. On the death of Mátyás Corvinus, the Hungarian crown passed to kings of the Polish Jagiellonian dynasty, who were forced to devolve many of their powers to the nobles. These lords fought among themselves, dismantled the royal administration and, in 1514, goaded the peasants into an abortive uprising that was suppressed at the cost of 50,000 lives. The leaders were tortured to death and their followers were punished by the assembly of nobles known as the "Savage Diet," which passed ferocious decrees binding the

A NATION DISMEMBERED

In the late 18th century, the Republic of Poland disappeared from the political map of Europe, swallowed in three bites by its neighbors. In 1772, after jointly quelling a Polish uprising, Russia, Austria and Prussia agreed to annex large tracts of land on the republic's frontiers, saying that anarchy threatened the region's stability. By 1793, still unsatisfied, Russia and Prussia claimed that the republic was a breeding ground for radicalism. Their remedy: another amputation of Polish territory. A popular revolt followed. Russia and Prussia sent armies to quash the violence and, with Austria, divided the remainder of the republic among themselves in 1795.

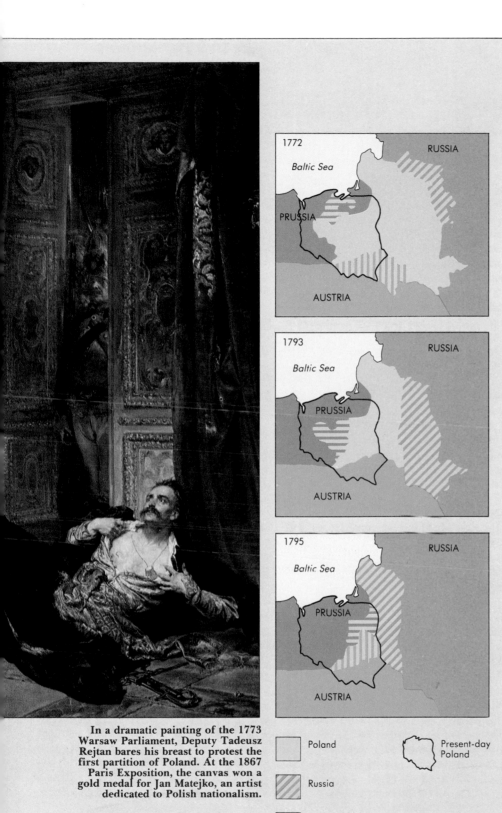

In a dramatic painting of the 1773 Warsaw Parliament, Deputy Tadeusz Rejtan bares his breast to protest the first partition of Poland. At the 1867 Paris Exposition, the canvas won a gold medal for Jan Matejko, an artist dedicated to Polish nationalism.

1772
Baltic Sea
RUSSIA
PRUSSIA
AUSTRIA

1793
Baltic Sea
RUSSIA
PRUSSIA
AUSTRIA

1795
Baltic Sea
RUSSIA
PRUSSIA
AUSTRIA

Poland

Russia

Prussia

Austria

Present-day Poland

peasants to the soil and committing their lives to the authority of "their natural lords."

An impoverished and demoralized Hungary was no match for the tough, well-equipped army of the young Turkish Sultan Suleiman the Magnificent, who came to power in 1520. The all-important fortress of Belgrade fell into his hands in 1521, but he postponed the final assault on Hungary for another five years: He was busy conquering Egypt and besieging Rhodes. The Magyar nobles failed to take advantage of the breathing space and refused to provide their young king, Louis II, with the funds needed for re-equipping the Hungarian army. When Suleiman and his host of 300,000 finally marched on Hungary, they met the 20-year-old Louis and some 25,000 poorly armed nobles on the plain of Mohács—and slew the king, his commanders, and all but 1,000 of his followers in a battle lasting only two hours. Suleiman could hardly bring himself to believe that the pitiful force he had just destroyed represented the national army of Hungary.

The victorious Turks fanned out through the country, looting, burning, and slaughtering about 200,000 people. Suleiman seized the citadel of Buda and loaded his river vessels with Mátyás Corvinus' collection of jewels, statues, rare books, paintings, and objects wrought of gold and silver. More than 100,000 captives were sent into slavery, along with a vast amount of spoil that filled the bazaars of Istanbul for months to come.

After 500 years of flourishing existence, the Kingdom of Hungary ceased to be an independent state. The country was eventually divided into three parts. The territories of the north and west—"Royal Hungary"—fell under the control of Ferdinand of Hapsburg, who ruled the German Empire from Vienna. The central area, including the twin cities of Buda and Pest—"Turkish Hungary"—was occupied by the Ottomans. Transylvania became a small independent principality, allowed to survive as long as it remained a satellite of the Turkish empire.

The Turkish occupation of Hungary lasted a century and a half, from 1541 to 1699. During these years, the political consequences of the Reformation were fought out in the lands to the north and west, on the battlefields of the Thirty Years' War. Significantly, the great bloodletting began in Bohemia, where Protestant nobles refused to accept the Catholic Ferdinand of Hapsburg when they were asked to vote on the succession in 1618. Instead, some of them perpetrated the Second Defenestration of Prague by throwing two Catholic governors and their clerk from the windows of Prague Castle into the moat below. The victims fell onto a heap of rubbish and escaped from Prague to tell their story in Vienna; but as an act of treason, the defenestration proved sufficient to precipitate the many-sided struggle that soon involved most of the great powers of Europe.

The Bohemian Protestant army was routed at the Battle of the White Mountain in 1620. This time, rather than attempt a reconciliation, the Hapsburgs were determined to eradicate Czech Protestantism once and for all. Twenty-six Protestant leaders and a Catholic who had joined them were mutilated and beheaded for treason in front of the Prague town hall. The property of the Protestant nobles was confiscated; serfs and the lower orders were forcibly converted; the nobles and middle classes were given the choice of conversion

or expulsion. Some 300,000 people, including large numbers of artists and scholars, fled the country, never to return. For the next 300 years, Bohemia and Moravia ceased to have an independent existence and figured as a province and "crownland" of the Hapsburg Empire. Moreover, in the prevailing zeal to stamp out the spirit of resistance, Czech books were burned en masse by the Jesuit censors, and Czech ceased to be a literary language.

For decades, the war raged in the surrounding lands as armies of mercenaries plundered their way through the states of central Europe. Only when both sides were thoroughly exhausted and it became apparent that neither could win did the Catholics and Protestants agree to compromise their interests at the Peace of Westphalia in 1648. Poland had remained on the sidelines and escaped the full horrors of the conflict. But just as the peace treaty came into force, the country was wracked by a civil war—the great Cossack rebellion of 1648, when the savage horsemen of the Ukraine rose in revolt.

Under their daring leader, Bogdan Chmielnicki, the Cossacks made short work of the regular Polish army and indulged in a reign of terror in which the Polish gentry of the Ukraine were butchered, flayed and burned alive. The revolt took on the trappings of an Orthodox crusade against Roman Catholics and Jews, thousands of whom were tortured and killed during the course of Chmielnicki's victorious march on Kiev. The newly elected king, Jan Kazimierz, had no choice but to accede to a truce that recognized the rebel leader as prince of a virtually autonomous Ukraine. In 1654, Chmielnicki took the oath of allegiance to the tsar of Muscovy, the Cossacks' ally

against the Poles. The stage was set for a major shift in the balance of power between Poland and Muscovy, which now styled itself "Great Russia." Thirty years later, the Ukraine was formally annexed by the Russian tsar.

The loss of the Ukraine was indicative of the progressive weakening of Polish power. Yet shortly afterward, a new and more dynamic ruler, Jan Sobieski, performed one of the great feats of Polish military history when he raised the siege of

Vienna in 1683. The Ottoman Turks had revived their dream of establishing a Western Muslim empire in the heart of Europe, and their first objective was the heavily fortified city of Vienna. For two months, a force of nearly 300,000 Turkish troops under the Grand Vizier Kara Mustafa besieged the city, hoping to starve out its defenders. The Hapsburg Emperor Leopold I had fled, leaving behind him a garrison of 34,000 men with firm orders to hold out at all costs.

Although the interests of Poland and

Austria had frequently clashed, Jan Sobieski went gallantly to the Austrians' rescue with a hastily raised army of 26,000 men and 29,000 horses—including 25 regiments of Polish hussars and 77 Cossack troops. With these fast, fierce riders, Sobieski swooped down on the Turks in their giant tent city, taking them completely by surprise. The entire force—the mighty 300,000—fled in panic. "All the guns, the whole camp, untold spoils have fallen into our hands," he wrote to his queen, Marysieńka, after the battle. "There is enough powder and ammunition alone for a million men. The vizier took such hurried flight that he only had time to escape with one horse, and in the clothes he wore. . . . I have all his personal insignia, which were borne before him, and the Mahometan banner, which his emperor gave him for the war."

Jan Sobieski's troops also acquired an enormous store of coffee, left behind by the Turks. This was sold for a pittance to a local merchant, who used the windfall to open the first coffeehouse in Vienna.

The victor was persuaded to join the Austrians and their allies in a protracted campaign against the still-powerful Turks. In so doing, however, Jan Sobieski dissipated his military strength just when it was needed to safeguard Polish interests against an increasingly imperialist Russia. After Sobieski's death, the kingdom fell into such disarray that the prince-elector of Saxony, Augustus the Strong, was able to bribe the Polish nobles into electing him to the throne in 1697. Augustus' real interests were not Polish, but Saxon and dynastic. During the 70 years he and his son Augustus III held power, they did little to halt the transformation of Poland into a Russian protectorate.

Internally, the country was divided by perpetual feuding among the great families, such as the Potocki, the Czartoryski, the Lubomirski and the Radziwiłł. Many of these families owned estates that occupied thousands of square miles and ran them as all-but-independent states. Periodically, these lands became battlegrounds as Russian, Swedish, Prussian and Saxon troops cut swaths of devastation across the Polish countryside. After several such wars, it was clear that Russia had emerged as the predominant power of Eastern Europe. After the death of Augustus III in 1763, there was nothing to prevent Russia, Austria and Prussia from dismembering Poland—a three-stage process effected in 1772, 1793 and 1795.

The partitioning of Poland coincided with the reign of the nation's last king, Stanisław August Poniatowski, who could only watch helplessly while Poland was "consumed leaf by leaf, like an artichoke," as Frederick the Great of Prussia had foreseen. The pretext for this unprecedented dismantling of a sovereign state was that Polish anarchy threatened the peace of Europe. Furthermore, the partitioning powers possessed territorial rights and claims "as ancient as they are legitimate."

Meanwhile, not only Poland but all

Europe was seething with discontent. When the French Revolution overturned the ancien régime in Versailles, a group of Polish patriots under Tadeusz Kościuszko (who had fought with distinction in the American War of Independence) started a revolution of their own. During the spring and summer of 1794, the Polish revolutionary army achieved a string of surprising victories over the Russian and Prussian forces that took the field against them. But theirs was clearly a lost cause: By November, the last Polish army corps was forced to capitulate. In the final partition, Austria annexed 18 percent, Prussia about 19 percent and Russia approximately 63 percent of the Polish-Lithuanian state as it had been in 1772.

One result of the third partition was that thousands of Poles emigrated to Western Europe, and some of them ended up fighting for the French Republic and in the armies of Napoleon. The self-made emperor of the French created several Polish legions that were commanded by the best of the Polish generals, such as Józef Poniatowski and Henryk Dabrowski. In 1807, following his victory over Prussia and Austria, Napoleon revived Polish hopes of independence by carving the Duchy of Warsaw out of the territory of Prussian Poland—but the state was far too small and weak to gain autonomy. There were nearly 100,000 Poles in Napoleon's Grande Armée when the emperor invaded Russia in 1812; for them it was a war of liberation. But only 20,000 Polish men survived the destruction of the French army during the retreat from Moscow.

When the map of Europe was redrawn at the Congress of Vienna in 1815, the Duchy of Warsaw was replaced by another political entity.

Marshal Józef Piłsudski, Polish soldier and statesman, wrested his homeland from more than a century of foreign domination at the outset of World War I. He offered military support to Germany and Austria in exchange for Poland's independence.

There was to be a new, independent Kingdom of Poland, known as the Congress Kingdom; but its crown was to be worn by the tsar of Russia. Under this arrangement, the Polish nobles were initially permitted to run their own domestic affairs, albeit under a Russian governor with his own troops.

In 1830, however, public discontent with Russian repression reached a flash point, and a group of impetuous revolutionaries launched a badly prepared insurrection that became known as the November Rising. The ensuing war between the Poles and the Russians lasted until the following September, when the armies of Tsar Nicholas I entered Warsaw and began the terrible work of retribution. The leaders of the revolt were executed. Thousands of captured rebel officers were deported to Siberia; ordinary soldiers were conscripted into the Russian army and sent to the Caucasus. Revolutionaries who succeeded in escaping abroad learned that their families had been arrested and deported in their stead.

In the aftermath of the rising, a huge army of occupation was installed in the Congress Kingdom at Polish expense, and the last institutions symbolic of Polish self-rule were abolished. Henceforth, Russian Poland was ruled by tsarist decree. Yet the idea of liberation was kept alive by the fervent literary and artistic nationalism of exiles such as the composer Frédéric Chopin, whose polonaises taught the rest of the world something about the pride and courage of his countrymen, and the poet Adam Mickiewicz, whose poetry described, among other things, the terrible plight of the deported families:

Poor boys! The youngest only ten years old,
Complained he couldn't lift his heavy chains
And showed his foot all flecked with blood and bare.
The captain then rode up to see this—
So kind and just, himself would test the chains!
"Ten pounds, quite right; that is the weight prescribed."

Throughout the 19th century, as the modern Industrial Revolution was transforming the face of Europe, Poland, Bohemia and Hungary were being ruled by foreign monarchs whose chief concern was to preserve the political status quo and to prevent any resurgence of nationalist feeling. Even so, the latent energies of all three countries proved irrepressible. Their major cities gradually became important commercial centers, and industrial production slowly began to rival agriculture as a primary source of national wealth. Poland, though oppressed by the tsars, vastly expanded its industries and developed a thriving economy based on steel mills, textile weaving, and a range of consumer products.

Bohemia became the most important industrial province of the Hapsburg Empire. The leading industries of Bohemia and Moravia included iron and steel, agricultural machinery, railroad rolling stock, chemicals, armaments, glass and porcelain. Hungary, the breadbasket of the empire, was slower to acquire modern industries, but it, too, became an important producer of ceramics, tools, paper, leather goods and woolen cloth.

However, the onward march of the Industrial Revolution only accelerated the drift toward political revolutions. Hungary, led by Lajos Kossuth, rose against the Hapsburgs in 1848—a year of revolutions throughout the Continent—but the revolutionary army was crushed by Russian troops sent by Nicholas I to help the Austrians.

The lyric poet Sándor Petőfi, only 26 years old but a major in the revolutionary army, was killed in a battle with the Russians at Segesvár in July 1849. It was an age of romantic heroes: Legend says that Petőfi still lives and will rise again to help his nation in a future hour of need. The Petőfi saga inspired the Hungarian composer Franz Liszt to write a piano piece in his memory. It was one of a number of patriotic works—not least the *Hungarian Rhapsodies*—in which the French-educated Liszt rediscovered his own Magyar heritage and created a Hungarian furor in the world's concert halls.

The Czechs staged a briefer revolt in June 1848, when workers and students took to the barricades in the streets of Prague. The local Austrian commander, Prince Windischgrätz, whose wife was killed by a stray bullet in their home in the center of Prague—withdrew his troops and bombarded the city. After six days, Prague capitulated unconditionally. And for several years, the Austrian authorities banned the use of Czech in schools and newspapers; again German became the official language of Bohemia.

And so the task of giving expression to national feelings and aspirations fell to composers such as Bedřich Smetana and Antonín Dvořák, who became international spokesmen for a nation not supposed to speak its own language. "Music is the life of the Czechs," Smetana declared, and he enshrined his ardent nationalism in a famous cycle of symphonic poems, *Má Vlast (My Country)*, that depicted the historic sites and magnificent landscapes of Bohemia. Smetana went deaf on the very day that the heroic opening theme of the "Vyšehrad" section came to him. For the rest of his life, he was unable to hear a note, though he went on to complete his symphonic poems and many other important scores. "I have never heard the greater part of my poetic creations," Smetana wrote toward the end of his life, "but I have seen many times how most of the people in the audience wept as they listened to the music I composed!"

During the last third of the century, it was clear that the power of the Hapsburgs was waning, especially after they lost a short war against Prussia in 1866. Franz Josef was forced to make major concessions, particularly to the restive Hungarians. In 1867, after years of effort and negotiation by Ferenc Deák, a leading Magyar statesman, the empire was formally divided into two parts, Austria and Hungary. Franz Josef was to reign over both nations—as emperor of Austria and king of Hungary—but there were to be separate parliaments and ministries, with the exception of those for defense, finance and foreign affairs. That very year, Franz Josef was crowned Apostolic King of Hungary—to the music of a coronation mass by Liszt, whose music until then had favored the revolutionaries.

Franz Josef, however, knew how to make amends gracefully. During the coronation he declared solemnly that he wished "a veil to be drawn over the past." The usual coronation gifts were donated to a fund for invalid veterans of the revolution. The new Hungarian constitution satisfied the Magyars but alarmed the many minority groups living within the borders of Greater Hungary—among them Rumanians, Ruthenians, Slovaks, Croats, Slovenes and Italians—who were subjected to the full force of Magyar nationalism and eventually forced to conduct most of their official business in the Hungarian language.

The Czechs also demanded an autonomous kingdom, but they had to settle for half a loaf, or rather a "policy of breadcrumbs," as the radicals called it. Under the new dispensation, the Czech language was reinstated in schools and could again be employed in official documents. Student agitation led to a division of the ancient University of Prague into separate Czechoslovakian and German faculties. Still, the language problem continued to cause violent friction between Czechs and Germans. The latter constituted only 30 percent of the electorate in Bohemia, yet they succeeded in paralyzing the regional parliament and in dominating the imperial government's policies toward the Czechs.

In any case, the political strategems and compromises that had held the Hapsburg Empire together since the Congress of Vienna were no longer working: Many people thought it was merely a matter of time before the whole tottering structure came down with a crash. In 1908, the Hapsburgs achieved one final piece of territorial aggrandizement when they annexed the Ottoman provinces of Bosnia and

Herzegovina in present-day Yugoslavia. Attending military maneuvers in the region six years later, the Archduke Franz Ferdinand, heir to the throne, was assassinated by a Serb patriot. The shots fired at Sarajevo on June 28, 1914, plunged all of Europe into war.

Even though the Austro-Hungarian army boasted some of the most elegantly uniformed officers in Europe, it was badly equipped and poorly led. Ironically, it was hampered by the language problem: Some of the German-speaking officers could not communicate easily with their Czech or Slovak conscripts. Czech soldiers were not at their best, in any case, when sent to fight against fellow Slavs on the Russian front.

Jaroslav Hašek's famous book, *The Good Soldier Švejk*, relates the adventures of a brilliantly stupid Czech malingerer in the imperial army who follows every order to the letter and manages to do little or nothing at all. Indeed, tens of thousands of "Švejks" surrendered or deserted to the enemy as soon as they had the chance. Later in the war, when the Czech independence movement had found support among the Allied powers, it was arranged for volunteers among the prisoners to be formed into a Czechoslovak army corps. All told, some 130,000 Czechs and Slovaks fought with the French, Italian and Russian armies.

At the peace conferences following the collapse of the Central Powers—Germany, Austria-Hungary, Bulgaria and Turkey—the map of Europe was again drastically redrawn, this time in accordance with a vaguely defined principle of self-determination. Poland was resurrected; Austria was severed from

2

Hungary, and both were truncated; Czechoslovakia and Yugoslavia came into being; Finland became independent of Russia; Lithuania, Latvia and Estonia appeared as republics on the Baltic. Yet for one reason or another, none of the newly established states was wholly satisfied with the outcome, and it soon became clear that political independence was not a panacea for the myriad problems of Eastern and central Europe.

The German government had proclaimed a new Polish state during the war, but only as a propaganda device. Polish independence did not become a reality until the state received the support of the victors at Versailles in 1919; its new frontiers were not finally settled until 1921, after the Poles had fought a series of border wars—with Germany, Lithuania, Czechoslovakia, and Soviet Russia—to validate their claims.

The most important factors in the confused political situation confronting Poland's postwar leader, Marshal Józef Piłsudski, were the Russian Revolution and the transformation of tsarist Russia into the Bolshevik-led Union of Soviet Socialist Republics. Though still struggling with internal disorder and international ostracism, Lenin's Russia was strong enough to attempt a reconquest of Poland with an army of 700,000 men.

The Russians advanced as far as the outskirts of Warsaw, where Piłsudski's forces brought the Red Army to a standstill. Lenin conceded defeat, and the Russo-Polish treaty of 1921 drew Poland's eastern frontier along a meandering line that took in both Wilno and Lwów. The young nation's tentative democracy, however, was soon faced with enormous social and economic problems. Piłsudski, who had

A lone church steeple rises above the rubble of Warsaw, a city systematically leveled by the Nazis in retribution for its 63-day uprising in 1944. In just over two months, they destroyed 85 percent of the city, including 782 historic sites. Rebuilding began shortly after the Soviet army arrived.

gone into retirement, took over as dictator after a right-wing coup in 1926; and following his death in 1935, Poland was governed by a military junta known as the "regime of colonels."

Much the same political evolution took place in Hungary, which was less than half its former size. As a result of the Treaty of Trianon, Hungary lost 68 percent of its prewar territory and 59 percent of its population—mostly to Rumania, Czechoslovakia and Yugoslavia, but also to Austria, Poland and Italy. Of the 10 million people who spoke Magyar as their mother tongue according to the 1910 census, more than 3.2 million occupied areas outside the borders of the new Hungary. After the failure of a short-lived experiment with Communism under a government headed by Béla Kun, Hungary made an abrupt turn to the right. The new state was declared a "monarchy with a vacant throne" and acquired a regent, Admiral Miklós Horthy, who governed with dictatorial powers until the outbreak of World War II.

Czechoslovakia, on the other hand, now developed a genuinely democratic government and a series of successful republican institutions. It was formed by joining the Czech Lands—Bohemia and Moravia—to the territories of Slovakia and Ruthenia, which had been under Hungarian rule. These boundaries created almost as many ethnic and linguistic problems as they resolved, for the new nation consisted of 46 percent Czechs, 28 percent Germans, 13 percent Slovaks, 8 percent Magyars and 3 percent Ruthenians. Fortunately, along with a quarter of the population and a fifth of the territory of the old Austro-Hungarian monarchy, Czechoslovakia had inherited fully two thirds of the empire's industrial capacity and

was thus economically viable from the very beginning.

One of Czechoslovakia's greatest assets was its first president, Tomáš Masaryk, a distinguished intellectual and politician who had gone into exile in France in 1914 to become the chief spokesman for Czech independence. At the end of the war, he returned to liberated Prague as head of the state at the age of 69. He was determined, as one historian put it, to "create an island of democracy in the center of Europe": He was a liberal and an idealist who believed that the Czechs could prevail "just by working hard, loving music, and being tolerant and reasonable." Yet after less than 20 years, Masaryk's achievements were destroyed by a rearmed, expansionist Germany led by Adolf Hitler.

In 1938, the allies on whom Czechoslovakia relied for security, France and Great Britain, gave Nazi Germany a free hand in central Europe—ostensibly in the hopes of preserving what British Prime Minister Neville Chamberlain called "peace in our time." First the German-populated Sudeten territory, then Czechoslovakia as a whole, was occupied by Hitler's forces. Bohemia and Moravia were incorporated into the Third Reich as a *Protektorat;* only Slovakia was permitted a nominal independence as a Nazi-controlled puppet state.

German troops marched into Prague on March 16, 1939; less than six months later, Germany started World War II with a *Blitzkrieg* invasion of Poland. When nearly all of western Poland had been occupied by the Germans despite stiff resistance, Soviet troops crossed the border and seized the eastern half, in accordance with the secret provisions of a treaty between

2

Hitler and the Soviet dictator, Josef Stalin, that had been drawn up in Moscow a month earlier. This was yet another partition of Poland, and again the state ceased to exist.

Under its new overlords, both halves of Poland were subjected to unspeakable atrocities. Conditions grew even worse when Hitler's forces invaded Russia in 1941, advancing almost to the gates of Leningrad and Moscow. According to the Führer's "geopolitical" program, occupied territories were to be Germanized and their Slavic populations either annihilated, resettled in Siberia, or turned into serfs for German colonists. But the first to experience the full horror of the Hitler regime were the Jews and gypsies of Europe. Of the estimated 40 million victims of World War II, 11 million, including six million Jews and two million gypsies, were killed in occupied Polish lands. They were murdered in the world's first death factories for human beings—at Auschwitz, Chełmno, Bełzec, Sobibór and Treblinka.

About half a million of these victims came from Horthy's Hungary, which had become a German ally and had sent its army to help Hitler invade Russia. As a reward, Hungary was permitted to reoccupy much of the territory it had lost to Czechoslovakia, Rumania and Yugoslavia. Early in 1943, however, the Hungarian army in Russia was virtually annihilated at Voronezh. Although the Hungarians tried desperately to conclude a separate peace with the Western Allies, it was the Red Army that entered Budapest in February of 1945, bringing with it a Soviet-sponsored Provisional Government of Democratic Hungary. In this way was postwar Hungary brought firmly into the Soviet sphere of influence. The peace treaty of 1947 formally restored the nation's prewar frontiers, although they were modified by a small border rectification in favor of Czechoslovakia—which had now, in turn, lost the whole of Ruthenia to the Soviet Union.

The Polish boundary changes at the end of the the war were far more extensive. The Soviet Union retained the eastern half of prewar Poland and "compensated" its new satellite by enlarging the western half with territory annexed from Germany. The new border between Germany and Poland ran along the Oder and the western Neisse—the so-called Oder-Neisse line, which was approved by Allied leaders at the Potsdam conference held in July and August of 1945. In the words of one commentator, it was as though Poland had been moved bodily 150 miles to the west, "like a company of soldiers taking 'two steps to the left, close ranks.' " To make room for Polish settlers coming in from the east, the German inhabitants of Silesia and other former German territories were forced to leave their homes and flee westward to become displaced persons in what remained of Germany. When the process had been completed, the new People's Republic of Poland comprised about four fifths as much territory as its predecessor, but its population had fallen by one third.

The people of the Soviet Union had borne the brunt of Hitler's brutal and destructive war, and it was not surprising that the Russians were determined to exploit their victory and assert their power in postwar Europe. Accordingly, they took steps to protect their western approaches with a ring of satellite states that would do Stalin's bidding. As Britain's wartime leader, Sir Winston Churchill, noted in 1946, "From Stettin in the Baltic to Trieste in the Adriatic, an iron curtain has descended across the Continent."

In Warsaw, Prague and Budapest, remnants of parties other than those approved by the Soviets were soon eliminated from the political scene. The most difficult of the three to bring under Soviet control was Czechoslovakia, which had known democracy before the days of Hitler and whose democratically elected leaders made a concerted attempt to keep the country in the Western camp. These efforts came abruptly to an end early in 1948, when the liberal president, Eduard Beneš, was forced to resign and Jan Masaryk, the popular foreign minister and son of Tomáš Masaryk, fell or was pushed from a window—a "suicide" that became known as the Third Defenestration of Prague.

Yet hardly was the Communist regime firmly established in power when the world was treated to the curious spectacle of the revolution devouring its own children. After a show trial in 1952, the secretary general of the Czechoslovakian Communist party, Rudolf Slánský, and 10 other prominent party officials were executed on trumped-up charges. Many others received long prison sentences. Such measures became a familiar part of political life in the postwar Soviet bloc as Stalin's henchmen tightened their control of the local Communist apparatus. The whole of Eastern Europe breathed a sigh of relief when Stalin died in March of 1953, and conditions in Russia and the satellite countries improved markedly. Yet it also became clear that none of these countries would be permitted to opt out of the Warsaw Pact—the military alliance established in 1955, with the Soviet Union as decision

HUNGARY'S BITTER REVOLT

The 1956 Hungarian Revolution began quietly on October 23, with a silent demonstration organized by Budapest students against the Soviet military presence in Poland. Some 300,000 people—nearly half the citizenry between the ages of 20 and 40—filled the streets.

When a government security force fired into the crowd, the protest flared into a revolution. Hungarian troops ordered to subdue their outraged countrymen promptly joined the insurgents, tearing the red stars from their uniforms and distributing arms to the crowd.

As Soviet tanks, requested by party leader Gerő, rolled into Budapest the next day, the revolutionaries built barricades throughout the city. After six days of fighting, which spread to other towns, a cease-fire was signed and the troops withdrew.

All over the country, peasants returned to their confiscated lands. Political prisoners were released, and Hungary's Roman Catholic cardinal was reinstated in his palace. Suppressed political parties reemerged to form a coalition government.

On November 4, alarmed by the new regime's renunciation of the Warsaw Pact, Moscow sent in the army again. After 14 days of bitter fighting, Hungary's revolution was crushed.

With a steady gaze belying her 15 years, a Budapest schoolgirl levels a machine gun. Although citizens of all ages and classes joined the fighting against the Soviet army, the invading force of 150,000 men and more than 2,000 tanks overwhelmed them.

In a battle-torn Budapest street, boys hurl books on a bonfire. Soviet literature, representative of the hated Stalinist line imposed on Hungarian writers since 1949, was burned in vast quantities by the rebels.

A handful of Russian officers and men survey a subdued Budapest on November 12. The date marked the end of fighting in the city, but battles continued for several more days in the Hungarian countryside

maker and the rest as more or less willing participants.

From time to time, the countries of the Warsaw Pact have tried to assert their independence of the Soviet Union and to depose its surrogates. Discontent with the harshness of Communist rule has led to both violent uprisings and more subtle efforts to loosen the party's grip. In Hungary, when an exasperated population rose in open revolution in 1956, it was swiftly crushed by Soviet tanks. And in Czechoslovakia in 1968, Warsaw Pact tanks moved in, with an occupation army of 600,000 troops, to remind the Czechs that they had no alternative but to conform to Soviet standards.

In Poland, repeated outbursts from discontented workers and critical intellectuals have succeeded in exacting certain changes from the party leadership, though the essence of Communist rule has remained intact. But in the early 1980s, it was in the name of Polish patriotism rather than Communist ideology that the country's hastily installed new military leader, General Wojciech Jaruzelski, abolished the independent labor union, Solidarity, and its implied threat to Soviet hegemony. Although on this occasion the Soviet troops remained in their barracks, it was understood that open defiance by Polish dissidents would meet with the customary Soviet response.

As a result, the people of Poland, Czechoslovakia and Hungary are still searching for a means of obtaining more breathing space without arousing the anger or anxiety of their powerful Eastern neighbors. Whatever has changed in the 1,000 years of these nations' histories, the precariousness of their position—and their fierce pride in face of it—remains the same. □

Antonín Dvořák (1841-1904)

The son of a country butcher in a village north of Prague, Dvořák became famous as a composer in the classic tradition of Beethoven and Brahms. Yet he seemed happiest when working on Bohemian subjects, such as *The Wild Dove* and the *Slavonic Dances.* His best-known symphony, *From the New World,* was born of his time spent as a visiting professor in America. Landscapes always affected Dvořák musically. At Niagara Falls, the composer stood still for a long time watching the roaring waters and finally turned to a friend: "What a symphony in B minor that will be!"

LOVE SONGS TO A HOMELAND

Many of the greatest classical composers of patriotic music have come from Eastern Europe—notably Frédéric Chopin, with his *Polonaises,* and Franz Liszt, with the *Hungarian Rhapsodies.* Yet no country has had a more eloquent group of musical representatives than the Czech Lands, which gave rise to the romantic Bohemian nationalism of Bedřich Smetana and Antonín Dvořák, and to the passionately Moravian music of Leoš Janáček. During the 18th century, English music critic Charles Burney noted in his travel diary that the Bohemians were "the most musical people of Germany, or perhaps all of Europe."

Chafing under the rule of the Hapsburg emperors, the Czechs discovered that music could be a powerful means of expressing their patriotism. Smetana led the way by becoming a self-proclaimed nationalist composer in the 1850s, when he heard a German musician's insults about the Czechs' supposed lack of originality. That night, a friend testifies, Smetana swore to the starry heavens "that he would dedicate his entire life to his nation, to the tireless service of his country's art." Smetana's cycle of tone poems, *My Country,* about the splendors of the Bohemian landscape, and his exuberant peasant opera, *The Bartered Bride,* inspired Dvořák to compose folk operas and nature music of his own. Janáček, youngest of the three, devoted his life to collecting Moravian folk songs, which he used to create a brilliant new style. He, too, regarded music as a way of depicting the beauty of his homeland. "The life here in the meadow is for them a paradise," he once wrote while watching children playing in a field. "I want to preserve a picture of a single afternoon with something more faithful than mere words—with notes!"

The pine forests near Dvořák's country home—Vysoka, near Příbram south of Prague—are carefully tended today by the state forestry service. Dvořák, who composed *From the Bohemian Woods,* was a passionate birder and taught his pupils that thrushes and other songbirds were the real music masters.

63

SMETANA'S BELOVED RIVER

The Vltava, which flows through Prague, inspired Smetana to write his finest symphonic poem—which has become better known to concert audiences by the river's German name, *Die Moldau.* The opening theme of his flowing, romantic score came to him one day as he was sitting beside one of the river's tributaries. But he was never to hear a single note of this or any of the other tone poems in his cycle *Má Vlast (My Country),* since he went deaf before completing it. In 1882, when all six sections of the work were performed in Prague, the concert turned into a patriotic rally. Smetana was greeted by a storm of applause that he could not hear, and hundreds of listeners lined up to shake his hand.

Bedřich Smetana (1824-1884)

About 85 miles south of Prague, the Vltava flows over man-made rapids beside the deserted mill at

64

Hněvkovice, near Týn nad Vltavou. Here the country resembles the "emerald meadows and lowlands" of Smetana's program notes for *Vltava*.

Two shepherds herd their flock in the rolling hills of Liptovská Teplička in central Slovakia. Such people inspired Janáček's *Shepherds' Song* and *The*

JANÁČEK'S SINGING HILLS

Janáček was even more interested in Czech and Slovak folk songs than Smetana or Dvořák. The seventh child of a village schoolmaster, he was reared in the highlands of eastern Moravia, near the Silesian border. He studied organ and taught music in Brno before becoming famous as a composer. Early in his career, Janáček began collecting songs in remote villages. He believed that "each song contains an entire man; his body, his soul, his surroundings, everything. He who grows up among folk songs grows into a complete man." His own music, based on these songs, became increasingly daring in rhythm and harmony. He composed some of the most complex, electrifying scores in the Czech repertoire—such as the operas *Jenůfa* and *The Makropoulos Affair*.

Leoš Janáček (1854-1928)

Wolf's Track. "Their song is most strange," he noted once, "and seems to spread all over the hilltops."

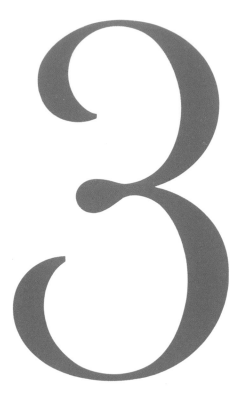

THE HUNGARIAN EXPERIMENT

A cyclist pedals past steep-roofed houses in the southern Hungarian village of Hajós. In a country where 70 percent of the arable land is cultivated, much of Hungary retains a lush and rural quality; almost one fifth of the nation's 10.7 million people still live in villages.

"What's the difference between socialism and your wife?" Hungarian men like to ask each other. "Nothing," comes the answer. "It's here, and it has to be loved." Of course, the joke is an expression of resignation—or, given Hungary's proximity to the Soviet Union, straightforward political realism. But it also marks a certain wry satisfaction that Hungary has made the "marriage" work, after a fashion.

Hungarians are very much aware that their country and its economic achievements are the nearest thing Eastern Europe has to a success story, and most of them are proud of it. Their capital of Budapest is by far the liveliest city in the Soviet bloc, seemingly free from the dead weight of cultural and economic repression: Its well-dressed, well-fed people have money to spend and Eastern Europe's widest range of consumer goods to spend it on. Posters are more likely to carry soft-drink advertisements than Marxist-Leninist exhortations, and in Hungary, lines form only at the checkout counters—not at the entrances—of bustling, well-stocked supermarkets.

Up to a point, individual enterprise is not only permitted but encouraged. Even official statistics admit that more than half the service economy is outside the "socialist sector." And private cars abound: one for every three households—a low proportion by Western standards and less, too, than in neighboring Czechoslovakia, but nonetheless a thirtyfold increase since 1960. And there are enough cars to give the weekend migration from Budapest to the waterside vacation homes and campgrounds of the resort area around Lake Balaton a density that is distinctly Western European. Many Hungarians travel a great deal farther afield: In 1985, for example, more than 5.5 million of the country's 10.7 million people took vacation trips abroad, 600,000 of them in the West.

Certainly, there are shortcomings in the system. The consumer goods that are the envy of Hungary's eastern neighbors are often expensive and of indifferent quality, and in any case they are not as readily available in the countryside, where half the population lives. A chronic housing shortage causes hardship for almost everyone, despite the out-of-town vacation homes that the wealthier have built themselves. Everyday life can often be complicated for the people of Hungary by a vast and intractably inefficient bureaucracy.

But on the whole, the country is prosperous, stable and almost contented. It is a description that stands in the most extraordinary contrast to the defeated, embittered and desperately unhappy nation of November 1956. At that time, after just a few exalted days of national rebellion, Soviet tanks and troops crushed freedom fighters and their hopes alike, killing several thousand Hungarians, deporting thousands more to Soviet concentration camps

69

3

and driving almost a quarter of a million people into exile across the Austrian and Yugoslav frontiers.

Hungary's socialist experience began in April of 1945, when the Red Army liberated the country from German troops and their Hungarian-fascist allies after a desperate, last-ditch defense that left little but rubble of some Hungarian cities. In their baggage trains, the Soviets brought with them Mátyás Rákosi, leader of the tiny Hungarian Communist party, who was later described as "Stalin's best disciple." But the Communists had only minority support in the country, and despite the presence of large numbers of Soviet troops, it was not until 1949 that Rákosi was able to set up a Hungarian People's Republic on the Soviet model, with himself at its head.

Once in power, Rákosi earned his reputation. Agriculture was ruthlessly collectivized, industry was nationalized, and an encompassing Five Year Plan was set in motion. Opposition was dealt with in the finest Stalinist traditions, by a state security police force—the infamous AVO—whose record for midnight arrests, brutal interrogations and cellar executions was second to none. Almost from the beginning, Rákosi indulged himself in purges of his own party, staging show trials in the Moscow fashion that decimated the senior membership and gave many of the future Hungarian leaders—including János Kádár, the country's ruler from 1956 into the 1980s—a firsthand inside view of a Communist jail.

Industrial production went up, but the standard of living did not. And so it was a worn-out, hungry and frightened population who listened, stunned, to the news in March 1953

Shoppers in Budapest throng the city's most modern department store, the Skála-Metró; in the background rise the offices of the Hungarian state railroad. The store is one of 64 retail outlets run by Skála-Co-op, a consortium founded by 300 agricultural and manufacturing cooperatives in 1975.

that Stalin himself, Rákosi's master and mentor, had died in Moscow.

In the leadership vacuum that now followed, Soviet control appeared to relax. Not all Hungarian Communists were in the Rákosi mold, and in July, he was replaced by the relatively liberal Imre Nagy. Nagy freed many of Rákosi's political prisoners, back-pedaled on collectivization and the huge investment being made in heavy industry and promised an increase in consumer goods. The ebb and flow of Kremlin politics after Stalin's death left Hungarian leaders completely dependent on Muscovite infighting; when Nagy's patrons lost, his reforms were doomed. In 1955, he was dismissed and expelled from the party. Rákosi was reinstalled, albeit with somewhat reduced powers, and the oppression began again.

But the brief Nagy interlude had raised hopes; it was harder to return to Stalinism. Rákosi was deposed once more a year later. This time the new Soviet leader, Nikita Khrushchev, ousted him, as much to humor Rákosi's old enemy, President Tito of Yugoslavia, as to appease the Hungarian people. And hopes rose once more. They were dashed when Rákosi's job went to his austere and unpopular henchman, Ernő Gerő.

By this time, though, the people had had enough. On October 23, 1956, student demonstrations in Budapest turned into a popular uprising—an uprising led, for the most part, by Communist intellectuals of the Nagy school and supported by almost everyone. When Gerő called for "fraternal assistance" from Soviet troops, the Hungarian army joined the rebellion and helped to provide arms for street-fighting workers. Soviet tanks sent to subdue the population were compelled to leave Budapest when attacks were made with hand grenades and so-called Molotov cocktails. Overnight, the whole Communist apparatus of Stalinist terror melted away. Gerő fled, and his hated AVO officers had to hide to save their lives. Some were later tracked down and lynched.

It was a heady, exuberant time, and for a while anything seemed possible. Imre Nagy was soon head of a coalition government that began to negotiate the withdrawal of Soviet troops from Hungary. For a few days, it seemed that he would succeed. On the 30th of October, the Soviet government admitted "violations and errors" and agreed in principle to depart. János Kádár, now

On a Budapest street, a smartly dressed shopper carries a single red gladiolus. Hungarians are extremely fond of flowers, and it is a custom—common throughout central Europe—for guests to present their hosts with blooms, either singly or in bunches containing an odd number.

out of prison and appointed first party secretary, broadcast to the nation to congratulate the people on their "glorious uprising." Allegedly, he also warned the Soviet ambassador (future Kremlin leader Yuri Andropov): "If your tanks enter Budapest, I will go into the streets and fight you with my bare hands."

But uplifted by the mood of popular exultation and fearing that the Russians would renege on their promises, the Nagy government went too far. On November 1, the premier denounced the Warsaw Pact and requested the United Nations to recognize Hungarian neutrality. The United Nations, of course, did nothing; and from the West came only expressions of admiration.

On November 4, the Russians were back in Budapest in full force, and the rebellion was over. In its place was a "revolutionary peasant-worker government" to be led by none other than János Kádár, who a few days before had disappeared mysteriously from Nagy's coalition cabinet. For the next two weeks, Kádár presided over one-sided strife in Budapest as Soviet army units flushed out the last of the rebels; fighting continued here and there in the countryside until the end of the year. Kádár seemed certain to go down in Hungarian history as the nation's greatest traitor. Instead, he was to lead his country to the highest level of prosperity it had ever known.

Few thought so in 1956. In all of Hungary's stormy history, the country had certainly been in worse physical shape; but the great lost expectations of the revolution had had a catastrophic effect on national morale. Nationwide strikes against the new government gradually died in the face of oppression from the Red Army and the revitalized security police; but tanks and guns could do nothing against the surly, foot-dragging mood that now affected almost everyone.

Kádár had come to power promising a continuation of reform, with no punishment for those who had taken part in "the great popular movement of the past few weeks." No one believed him, and no one was surprised when the arrests began early in 1957, when collectivization was reimposed, or when it was quietly announced, 18 months after "the great popular movement," that Imre Nagy had been hanged following a secret trial.

But Kádár was no Rákosi. The crazed brutality of the earlier regime was gone, and from the beginning, it was clear that he was ready to turn a blind eye to many deviations from strict socialism—provided, of course, that Communist power was never threatened. The collectivized peasants were allowed to retain private plots of land, and factory workers were no longer bullied. Kádár was also responsible for ending the attempts to bring Hungarian life under Soviet control. This had been less an ideological phenomenon than a simple-minded glorification of all things Russian, from clumsy fashions to grandiose industrial projects. It had always stuck in the throats of Hungarians, who had a passionately Magyar culture of their own and who had traditionally looked to the West for such inspiration as they needed.

Generally, people were prepared to be grateful for such small favors— and behind Kádár's rule was always the unstated implication that without him, Hungary would be in for something a good deal worse. It was probably quite true: After all, there were 60,000 Soviet troops stationed in the country to underline the point.

By 1960, Kádár felt strong enough to declare the first of several amnesties, and in 1962, he made a celebrated speech that gave his regime a rallying cry. If Rákosi's slogan had been "Those who are not with us are against us," said Kádár, then his own might be "Those who are not against us are with us."

The fact that the slogan had originally been coined as a sneer by an exiled opponent bothered the pragmatic Kádár not at all. The country was slowly but surely coming to life again. In 1968, his government gave Hungary its greatest boost so far, in the shape of the so-called New Economic Mechanism. The NEM did not aim so much to revive the private enterprise system—although that, too, was to be permitted in some small measure—as to revive enterprise itself. Production and marketing decisions were largely taken away from the officials of the state and were delegated to the managers of factories, cooperatives and farms. Efficiency was to be measured not in terms of fulfillment of state plans but in straightforward profit and loss, with many consumer prices being decided largely by market forces. Successful managers, and workers too, could expect to do well financially; the failures, conversely, would have to tighten their belts.

At the time of its introduction, the aims of the NEM bore some resemblance to reforms then being proposed in the Soviet Union. But the Soviet experiment foundered in a morass of entrenched bureaucratic power and sheer muddle. In Hungary, with its much smaller economy and shorter history of cumbersome state planning, the program worked very well. While Hungarian individuals got on with the job of

On the Danube River, a barge passes under one of the eight bridges that link the old towns of Buda (foreground) and Pest. Near the end of the war, Nazis blew up the city's fine bridges, but within 20 years all of them had been rebuilt.

enriching themselves, the state put more money into the national infrastructure, investing heavily in new roads, schools, hospitals and rural health-care centers, which did a good deal to improve everyday life in the less developed countryside.

Soon, the signs of modernization were ubiquitous. Spaceship-like water towers rose above almost every village, and television aerials sprouted everywhere. Cars and trucks still have not taken over completely from the horse and cart in the countryside, but the network of excellent roads built in the 1960s and 1970s has largely abolished the problems of rural isolation.

Social progress was also made. As the economy got into gear, the towns grew; Budapest in particular mushroomed until its megalopolis housed almost one fifth of the nation's people. The number of students in higher education increased more than threefold over the 1950 level, and there were more than twice as many doctors and one and one half times as many hospital beds per head of population.

In addition, a comprehensive welfare state developed, with profound effects on Hungarian society as a whole. Free education was provided for all children on an eight-year curriculum from the age of six or seven; 4 out of 5 students then went on to another four years at high school. As educational qualifications were the only social determinants sanctioned in Hungary's officially classless society, most parents' greatest wish was for their children to win places at the 70-odd universities and technical colleges that formed the top layer of the educational system, where nearly all students were supported in their tuition and living expenses by the state.

Health care, too, though not of a high quality, was free, paid for by employers' insurance contributions, and prescription medicines were available at heavily subsidized prices. Infant mortality rates decreased, and certain killer diseases that had formerly been endemic—notably tuberculosis and malaria—were eradicated. Large-scale programs of immunization against smallpox and polio and of screening for cancer were also undertaken.

Working conditions improved markedly from the prewar years. The concepts of job sharing and part-time work were officially sanctioned in 1979. Compulsory pension schemes, financed jointly by employer and employee contributions, covered the work force, and retirement was set at the relatively low ages of 60 for men and 55 for women. In the mid-1980s, the 40-hour, five-day work week was compa-

rable to that of many Western countries. The government officially claimed there was no unemployment; underemployment, however, was rife.

The state had less success in providing its citizens with homes. After the Communist takeover, housing was nationalized; but the construction of new units in the rapidly expanding towns soon failed to keep pace with demand. The low rents charged for state-owned housing bore little relation to the cost of maintaining the existing structures, let alone funding additional building. As a result, the government was forced to change its policy. In 1970, stiff qualifications were introduced for eligibility for public housing. More affluent Hungarians were encouraged, by preferential loans from the state and their employers, to form cooperative housing schemes—a compromise between public and private ownership.

A woman tries on a veil in a Budapest shop that rents wedding apparel (above). In the southern town of Makó (right), wedding portraits are displayed outside a photography studio. Most couples are married in civil ceremonies, but an increasing number opt for a church service as well.

The party, of course, was and still is firmly in charge. The various maneuverings by which Kádár got his reforms past Moscow's watchful eye became known as the *Kádár csárdás*, a political variation of the Hungarian folk dance that involved, cynics suggested, "two steps to the right and two steps to the left."

But Kádár always took care to explain to Moscow, in the peculiar coded jargon that Communist leaders like to use, exactly where his loyalties lay. He proved it in 1968, when he sent an unenthusiastic Hungarian army contingent to help in the Soviet invasion of Czechoslovakia. The messages he sent

to ordinary Hungarians, however, were equally clear, if rather different: Enrich yourselves by all means if you can—just stay out of politics.

"Rich" is a relative term. In 1986, the average Hungarian earned 6,540 forints a month—about $140. By comparison with any Western country, it is not an impressive amount. But since the costs of health, education and most other social services are heavily subsidized or free, the spending power it represents is not to be underestimated.

To earn their living, most Hungarians in the past worked the land. Massive postwar industrialization changed

all that, and by the mid-1980s, only 1 worker in 5 was employed in farming. Agriculture has nonetheless been one of Hungary's success stories in the 1980s, generating a quarter of the nation's exports and providing consumers with the best choice of foodstuffs in Eastern Europe. Just how this feat has been achieved makes an excellent illustration of the judicious style of the Kádár government.

Although the great majority of Hungarian farmland is still in the hands of the state, the existence of small private backyard plots that can be worked for profit is officially recognized. Indeed, most farm workers are now entitled to

3

the use of 1.5 acres as of right, and state aid in the form of fertilizers and animal fodder is made freely available to these people. The results of the policy have been startling. According to the Hungarian government's own 1984 statistics, the 3.7 percent of the land worked privately for profit added to the 6 percent of the land that is now in private hands produces slightly less than one third of the country's entire agricultural output and considerably more than one third of its meat.

The state sector, too, can claim its own success. The state farms themselves—no longer run by central planning agencies in the old bureaucratic manner—are tolerably efficient. Farming cooperatives, accounting for two thirds of the land and granted a large measure of economic autonomy by the 1968 reforms, have evolved in a remarkable manner. Making their own entrepreneurial decisions, many cooperatives have expanded, not just into related industries such as meat and vegetable canning, but also into plastic manufacturing, construction, and even hotels and restaurants.

Some have become big business indeed, and both their growth and their management style have done much to shape the Hungary of today. The "March 15" cooperative in the village of Hernád, about 30 miles from Budapest, is one example that demonstrates the unusual combination of capitalism and Communism that Hungary has used to enrich itself.

The cooperative was first set up in the dark days of 1958, when about 200 reluctantly collectivized peasants decided to go into chicken farming. "The land here is poor, and there was not much money," explains its president and chief executive, András Kele. "We

only went in for chickens because they were cheapest, and during the first years we sold them round the countryside as best we could."

Their chickens sold well, and the farmers branched out into pig farming and sausagemaking. In time, the cooperative was able to build its own slaughterhouse, thereby eliminating middleman costs. The 1968 reforms gave more scope for investment decisions, and soon the organization's income began to improve by leaps and bounds. Then the cooperative started to develop its own distribution system. "Business took off after we acquired a chain of shops in Budapest," said Kele. "Last year we earned almost $50 million."

The cooperative currently employs about 2,600 people—almost the entire working population of the area—of whom 1,200 are permanent members, people who have invested their savings in the organization and in consequence have full voting rights. "It's true that big, strategic decisions are still made at the highest level," Kele admitted. "But for all practical purposes, our leadership group is responsible to the cooperative at its annual general assembly. They elect us and they can dismiss us. There's no politics involved, though. In Hungary, you don't have to be a party member to lead a cooperative. You do have to be good at your job."

Enterprise in Hernád is not confined to the management team. Like most other cooperatives, "March 15" harnesses the efforts of the so-called private farmers—cooperative members with their own plots of land. "Private farmers do most of the chicken-raising. We lend them day-old chicks—the piglets, too—then buy them back when they're old enough for slaughter. It's a good interaction: It saves money for

the cooperative and it makes money for the farmers."

By Hungarian standards, it makes quite a lot of money for the farmers—as much as $1,500 in a good year, the equivalent of an extra annual salary earned in their spare time, for most of them also put in a full working day at the cooperative. Since many of them use the rest of their 1.5 acres for vegetable gardens or vineyards—a large proportion of Hungary's wine grapes are produced on private land—Hernád is beginning to show unmistakable signs of prosperity. Modern, standardized houses are mostly surrounded by ornate, expensive and highly individual fences, not to mention an extra pigsty or two tacked on at the back. The village has far more cars than Hungary's average rural community. Most cars are Russian-built Ladas or Czech Škodas, but here and there a nearly new Mercedes—prohibitively expensive in Hungarian terms—shows that its owner is not afraid to flaunt his wealth.

"They are all millionaires, here," confided one visiting—and envious—townsman. He was exaggerating, of course. But Hernád's people—like their counterparts elsewhere in Hungary—know a good life when they see it, and the government has little to fear from rural discontent. András Kele has no doubts about the reason for his community's success. "Without the cooperative it would be a disaster. If we returned to old-style private farms? Listen, if we gave the land back tomorrow, Hernád would be deserted in two days. Everybody would just pack up and leave."

In Hungarian industry, of course, there are no private businesses: A steelworker, for instance, can hardly run his

PRIVATE ENTERPRISE

An embroiderer displays her intricately stitched needlework.

A woman cradles a coypu raised in her backyard for its fur.

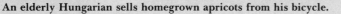
An elderly Hungarian sells homegrown apricots from his bicycle.

Pillows and cushions stand on show in a private garden.

Within Hungary's socialist system, small, profitable private enterprises coexist comfortably with the large state-run combines and cooperatives. In towns, villages and on agricultural collectives, Hungarians spend much of their spare time supplementing incomes or pensions by selling their own handicrafts, by raising animals for meat, milk or fur or by tilling small plots of land.

These plots, kept by an estimated 1.5 million families, rarely exceed 2.5 acres of ground, but in 1984, they provided almost 70 percent of the country's potatoes and vegetables, half its fruit and wine grapes, one fourth of the beef and dairy cattle and 40 percent of the poultry. More than half the pigs in Hungary were raised privately, helping to keep Hungary's larders stocked.

3

own blast furnace in the corner of his apartment. Many, however, do the next best thing: *maszek*. The term is a contraction of the Magyar words for "private sector" and the practice it describes. Only semilegal, but generally condoned by the authorities, *maszek* does much to explain the high standard of living that many Hungarians appear to enjoy despite the small monthly salaries they earn.

An official private sector does exist in Hungary, and its activities are noteworthy—about four fifths of the home-building industry, for example, is in private hands. But the word *maszek* is generally used to describe smaller-scale entrepreneurism. Bricklayers or mechanics, for instance, will employ their skills in their spare time to make a little extra money, undeclared to the authorities and hence tax free. Most workers with the opportunity will do private work on government time, too, using the state's materials, equipment and spare parts to make a quiet, personal profit for themselves.

Such activities are sometimes highly organized. In an enormous, state-owned automobile service center in Budapest, for example, the mechanics bustle about industriously during the day, progressing through their workload. At night, they work for themselves, without the tiresome paperwork the state has designed to keep things under control. Their customers pay more but get their cars back quickly, and the lucky few who can pay with hard cash often find that hitherto unavailable spare parts miraculously appear to hand.

"This is not a serious country," bemoaned a reasonably affluent Budapest intellectual, who had just paid about 800,000 forints, or about $16,475, to an unofficial work force to have his house renovated. "We Hungarians always spend more than we earn and yet we always seem to make ends meet." The primary reason, of course, is that the people who avail themselves of *maszek* goods and services are quite likely to be doing some *maszek* themselves, and the result is a highly developed submerged economy, built on a web of personal contacts and exchanged favors.

Some such arrangement exists in most countries, of course, East or West; the Hungarian version is chiefly remarkable for its extent. The very nature of the phenomenon makes accurate accounting impossible, but some estimates reckon that participating Hungarians make as much again from the unofficial economy as they do from the official one. And despite interfering occasionally, the authorities are generally content to let things be, for the situation is not without its advantages to them. *Maszek* individuals are always vulnerable to pressure: The illegal "privileges" that they enjoy can easily be withdrawn if they do not mind their political manners, without there being any need for the vast apparatus of police repression that existed in Stalinist days.

Certainly the system is a corruption of socialist ideas; but so were the Stalinist concentration camps. *Maszek* at least keeps people happy. Moreover, Hungary's under-the-counter economy is very different from the equivalent black market that operates in the Soviet Union. There, the clandestine sale of goods and services is the result of the endemic shortages created by centralized state planning. Shortages exist in Hungary, but to a much lesser extent than in the Soviet Union. *Maszek*

A large gaggle of geese gathers beside a farmhouse in the Hortobágy *puszta*, or prairie, of eastern Hungary. In this flattest and barest region of the Great Plain, stretching across some 270,000 acres, much of the landscape of heath and marsh is punctuated by irrigation works, farms and orchards.

896 Nomadic horsemen known as Magyars, or On-Ogurs—a Finno-Ugric people unrelated to the Slavs—establish themselves in the middle Danube basin at the heart of present-day Hungary; their chief, Prince Árpád, founds the country's first Magyar dynasty.

975 Árpád's great-grandson, Géza, is baptized into the Catholic faith.

1001 Géza's son, Stephen, is crowned the first Christian king of Hungary on Christmas Day *(crown, above)*. He forcibly converts his subjects to Christianity, builds churches, endows monasteries and creates the basis of a feudal state. (Stephen dies in 1038 and is canonized as Saint Stephen in 1087.)

1077-1095 King László I brings greater stability to a state wracked by dynastic infighting. Hungary's borders are extended to include Croatia and Transylvania, while feudalism turns the hitherto free peasantry into serfs.

1222 The Golden Bull, a charter of national liberties, is issued by Andrew II.

1241 Mongol Tatars of the "Golden Horde" devastate Hungary.

1301 The Árpád dynasty comes to an end with the death of heirless Andrew III. Robber barons, brigands and nobles engaged in internecine battles reduce the state to anarchy; order is restored by Hungarian kings of the House of Anjou, Charles I and Louis I, the Great.

1387 Emperor Sigismund of Luxembourg is crowned king of Hungary; in 1419, he becomes king of Bohemia as well.

1396 Sigismund attempts to stop the growing threat of the Turks to Hungary but is defeated by them at the Battle of Nicopolis in Bulgaria.

1456 János Hunyadi, a Transylvanian lord, vanquishes the Turks at the Battle of Belgrade.

1458 Mátyás Hunyadi, son of János, is elected king of Hungary. During his 32-year reign, arts and learning flourish at the royal court in Buda; an efficient administration and a regular army are established, but heavy taxes burden the oppressed peasantry.

1514 A massive peasant rebellion led by György Dózsa is ruthlessly crushed.

1526 At the Battle of Mohács on the 29th of August, the Turkish army of Ottoman Sultan Suleiman II completely destroys a small Hungarian force under Louis II. The Turkish forces briefly occupy and loot Buda.

1541 The Turks occupy the city of Buda again and partition the country into three divisions: Royal Hungary (Croatia and north and west Hungary), which remains under the rule of the Hapsburgs; central Turkish-held Hungary; and a semiautonomous Transylvania.

1686 Buda is liberated from the Turks by Hapsburg troops, but subsequent Austrian rule results in even harsher oppression of the peasants.

1699 The Turks withdraw from Hungary and are replaced by the Hapsburgs.

1703 Ferenc Rákóczi II leads a major national uprising against the Hapsburgs. Initial French support is lost when Louis XIV sides with Austria; Magyar troops are forced to surrender in 1711.

1825 A Hungarian reform movement aimed at removing the ancient privileges of the nobility, improving the lot of the peasants and gaining national freedom begins to grow. The Hungarian Academy of Sciences is founded in the capital, Pest.

1848 Hungarian statesman Lajos Kossuth heads an anti-Hapsburg revolution in mid-March; the following August, Hungarian troops are defeated by tsarist forces that are sent to help Austria. Kossuth goes into exile and Hungary is subjected to harsh Hapsburg control.

1867 With the creation of the Dual Monarchy, Hungary is given a separate parliament and internal independence, although Franz Josef of Austria remains the king.

1873 The towns of Buda and Pest are amalgamated officially to form Budapest.

1906 The composer Béla Bartók *(below)* publishes his *Twenty Hungarian Folksongs,* based on folk themes.

1918 At the end of World War I, Hungary is proclaimed an independent republic; in 1919, a brief "Soviet Republic" led by Béla Kun is overthrown.

1920 A right-wing admiral, Miklós Horthy, is made regent of Hungary. In the punitive Treaty of Trianon drawn up by

the Allies, Hungary loses two thirds of its territory and 60 percent of its population.

1941 Hungary joins the Axis powers of Italy and Germany and sends a token military force to help Germany's attack on the Soviet Union. In December, Britain declares war on Hungary.

1944-1945 Nazi troops occupy Hungary. Seven months later, Horthy is removed and Ferenc Szálasi, leader of the fascist Arrow Cross movement, seizes power and unleashes a reign of terror, especially against Budapest's Jews. Soviet troops liberate Budapest in February 1945.

1949 Hungary is declared a People's Republic, led by Mátyás Rákosi.

1956 A national Hungarian uprising is crushed by Soviet troops, and a new government is set up by János Kádár.

1959-1961 Privately held farmlands are collectivized to provide the core of Hungary's agricultural output.

1968 The "New Economic Mechanism" decentralizes production and allows limited private enterprise.

1972 Hungarian authorities license the first joint business ventures with Western partners to bring foreign capital and technology into the country.

1981 Hungarian designer Ernő Rubik's cube puzzle *(below)*, becomes the world's best-selling toy.

1986 Hungary joins the International Monetary Fund and the World Bank. The currency, the forint, is allowed to move freely on a daily basis against Western currencies.

is more a genuine wealth-creating economy than a black market because it increases spending power.

Hungary's government-controlled industry, on which the whole *maszek* system ultimately depends, has made progress. The original Soviet-style industrialization of the Rákosi years, which concentrated on steel and heavy engineering, was not well suited to Hungarian needs. But it did tilt the balance in what had previously been essentially an agricultural country. Since then, however, there has been a great deal of diversification, especially after 1968, when the technocrats and managers needed by every modern economy were given free rein as well as cash incentives. And there has always been one incentive that has nothing to do with government policy: Because it does not have its own natural resources—especially fuels—Hungary must export or die.

The need to export has led to a concentration on medium to high technologies geared to the international market, and trade with the capitalist West is increasing fast. By the mid-1980s, exports to the Communist bloc—once the overwhelming majority of all foreign sales—had dwindled, and Hungary's hard currency earnings were the envy of the neighboring countries. The Ikarusz bus, for example, is an international success: More than 90 percent of the buses are exported. The same is true of Medicor's medical equipment; and a surprising number of the so-called designer clothes that are sold in Western nations under famous labels turn out to have been manufactured under license somewhere in Hungary. A promising computer software industry is now developing, and Budapest can boast a growing number of small cooperative concerns that are engaged in the lucrative business of software production.

Hungary's best "small is beautiful" success story, however, comes from the 1970s, when a Budapest mathematics professor named Ernő Rubik invented an engaging little teaching aid designed to help his students. Rubik's cube sold by the tens of millions all over the world and started an international craze that amassed a fortune for its inventor. In true Hungarian style, however, Rubik still lives unostentatiously, teaching as he did before at the city's Academy of Applied Arts.

Hungary has another kind of trade, too, to bring in foreign currency: tourism. The dimensions of this asset are considerable: In 1985, the number of visitors almost matched Hungary's own population of just under 11 million. Most of these visitors came from Soviet-bloc countries, but the number coming from Western nations is steadily rising—more than two million arrived in 1985, for example.

Easterners and Westerners alike are drawn by the same thing: Hungary is a beautiful country. Budapest—carefully rebuilt after its World War II devastation—was once known as "the Paris of the East." Although its nightlife is not quite what it was between the wars, it is still a lively place after dark.

For the more affluent tourist, Budapest has a few international-style nightclubs and even a casino—for gamblers who come supplied with cold cash, that is. But its restaurants are probably the best value in Europe—especially since 1978, when the government began selling franchises of state-owned establishments to private operators, a move that brought about a big im-

3

**On the gravelly drive of the Bábolna
Stud Farm in western Hungary, a
purebred Arabian horse shows off its
form. Founded in 1789, the state-
run farm specializes in crossing Ara-
bians with tougher Hungarian breeds
to provide animals for international
sporting events.**

provement in both food and service. Restaurants help to make the city particularly appealing for other Eastern Europeans. It is not by chance that a disproportionately large number of Eastern-bloc cultural conferences and party gatherings are staged in the Hungarian capital.

Eastern tourists also appreciate the relaxed political atmosphere that they find throughout the country. Westerners take the lack of heavyweight bureaucratic harassment and the general freedom of movement for granted: For Czechs, Poles, East Germans and Russians, Hungarian-style socialism comes as a breath of fresh air. Hungary has a particular appeal for East Germans. Many use the country as a place to rendezvous with West German relatives in a situation where they can enjoy a holiday together without having the feeling that members of some sort of secret police are forever looking over their shoulders. (Hungary still has plenty of secret police, but their methods these days are discreet and they are not interested in tourists.)

The Hungarian people are not overly fond of visitors from their fellow-socialist neighbor nations in the Soviet bloc. Part of the reason is the long history of national antagonisms in the area, greatly exploited during the Hapsburg era on the principle of "divide and conquer." But there are other causes for Hungarian disdain. Czech and Soviet tourists who have money indulge in frenzied shopping sprees, staggering back to their home countries with as much as they can carry. Many such "tourists" are not really tourists at all: Poles especially, spurred by the dismal state of their own economy, have earned a reputation as black marketeers and smugglers.

The tourist trade is not all one way, for Hungarians are avid travelers. Passports for foreign travel are generally easy to obtain and do not restrict their holders to the Soviet bloc. Most Hungarians stay behind the iron curtain, however; vacations are cheaper there and currency regulations are less strict. In any case, ever since the Treaty of Trianon, most of Hungary's neighbors have included a Magyar-speaking minority in their population, and often the motive for a journey is simply to visit relatives.

Those Hungarians who do want to head westward can usually do so with little formality and can rely on a privilege unique in Eastern Europe: the right to buy, legally, hard foreign currency. There is a snag, of course. The sums permitted are far from adequate, and the balance must be made up from the black market if a well-disposed relative is not available in the West. And such trips are possible only once every three years—a restriction that the government ascribes, probably with perfect honesty, to the shortage of hard currency rather than to any fear of possible ideological contamination.

Access to the outside world does provoke a certain amount of resentment: Hungarians know what they are missing, although there are few unqualified admirers of Western ways. People have not forgotten the words, and words alone, with which the West responded to the tragedy of their failed revolution, and the comparisons that Hungarians inevitably make put their own considerable achievements into a slightly humiliating perspective. Some are small things. Budapest's Váci Road is rightly regarded as Eastern Europe's most fashionable shopping street, in which state-controlled stores with untotalitar-

3

ian names such as *Adam and Eve* have window displays that attract strollers even on bitter-cold, dark winter nights. But Hungarians who have seen London's Bond Street or New York's Fifth Avenue or a major shopping center in any of a hundred Western cities come back home to notice their own shops' dowdy packaging, the unironed clothes that hang from gawky plastic mannequins, the lack of choice, the lack of genuine quality, and prices for luxury

goods that are sometimes startlingly high. "You have so much, and we have so little," they remark, ruefully, to Western guests.

More profoundly, Hungarians envy the freedoms taken for granted in Western nations. It is not that Hungary groans under a terrible weight of repression. But everywhere, in almost every activity, there is a sense of restriction, of certain things that cannot be done, a constant feeling that "they"—

relatively benignly, perhaps—are looking over one's shoulder all the time.

Hungarians are an enterprising people, and left to their own devices, there is no reason why their country could not match or even exceed the economic achievements of its close Western European neighbors. They have not been left to their own devices, however. History and geography have imposed on Hungary certain inescapable facts of political life. The country may be the

THE YOUNG PEOPLE'S RAILROAD

Most Hungarian children from 10 to 15 years old belong to the Communist party's youth organization, the Young Pioneers. With the intention of instilling socialist values in its members, the Young Pioneers offer youngsters leisure and sports events, summer camps and community service projects.

One of the most unusual jobs is running the red-coached Pioneer Railroad. Established in 1950, this 7.5-mile-long narrow-gauge railroad cutting through the Buda Hills outside Budapest is staffed almost entirely by children. They act as guards, signal operators, ticket collectors and stationmasters. Only the engineer is an adult. The railroad is a major tourist attraction and may be a first step for many toward a career in the state rail system.

Three uniformed Young Pioneers dispatch trains on the Pioneer Railroad.

most comfortable barracks, as the wry Budapest joke has it, but Hungary is still in the "concentration camp." Stalinism has vanished, but the system that imposed it is still intact, and Hungarians are aware that repression could return at any time.

As things stand, there is a semblance of electoral politics in Hungary: Since 1985, all elections for the National Assembly of the Hungarian People's Republic—Parliament—must by law offer a choice of candidates for each seat. Because the candidates must in advance declare their support for the Communist-controlled Patriotic People's Front, however, the reform does not mean much. But it is as far as the

present regime is likely to go, or would, perhaps, be permitted to go. Besides, there is no great pressure for overt political reform: No one has any desire to rock the boat.

No one with the power to do any rocking, that is. For not all Hungarians have gained from the Kádár years, and there are plenty of thorns in the generally rosy picture. The regime's relatively easygoing economic policies have made a few Hungarians wealthy, but many have been left in comparative poverty. Pensioners, for example, often have to get by on as little as $73 a month, and they have few opportunities for increasing their income by extra work on the side. Peasants on successful

collectives are able to count their chickens and their forints and go for a drive in the family car, but there are plenty of inefficiently managed collectives. In addition, there are about 650,000 people still living on isolated, tiny farmsteads known as *tanyas,* with precious little in the way of roads, social services or even money.

Industry has had its problems, too, especially in the early 1980s, when declining world trade squeezed most economies, including Hungary's. Massive borrowing from the West—more than three billion dollars between 1984 and 1986—eased the pressure a little. But Hungary was not helped in the 1970s when the Soviet Union increased

In Széchényi Square in central Pécs, the elaborate façade of a public building is fronted by a memorial commemorating the plague of 1710. The architecture reflects much of the town's 2,000-year history, including its Turkish past.

86

by an average of 10 percent per year the price of the oil on which the nation's industry depends. Such a move was probably inevitable, though many Hungarians are convinced it was Moscow's way of making them pay for their relative economic freedom. These problems brought about an attack of inflation, and many workers have seen the real value of their wages shrink for the first time in many years. Nor can all of them find relief through the *maszek* system: It is all very well for people to be willing to tack an extra, semilicit occupation on to their official jobs in order to get a little bit ahead, but work is not always available.

The surprisingly unegalitarian salary structure of Hungary's socialist state also causes some grumbling. The increased pay differentials that were an inevitable consequence of the New Economic Mechanism benefit those who collect the highest wages and the top bonuses; but for those whose pay remains at base level, the differentials have become a source of bitterness. By the mid-1980s, even official statistics showed that the top 5 percent of wage earners took home 80 times as much as the bottom 5 percent—a ratio comparable with that of most nonsocialist lands. But complaints are difficult to express in Hungary, where labor unions are simply party agencies and strikes are illegal.

"How do ordinary workers feel?" reflected a highly respected Budapest television journalist. "Frankly, I simply don't know anymore. And neither does the party: The gap between the top and the bottom in Hungary has grown too wide. It's ironic, really. The country's officially a workers' state, but it's the workers at the bottom who have nothing. No power, no money. Nothing."

Poverty is one cause of the chronic alcoholism that afflicts the country. According to government figures, "beverages and tobacco" account for more than 15 percent of an average household's spending, and most observers would put the actual proportion spent on alcohol even higher. Early-morning drunks are a commonplace sight in Budapest streets and more than commonplace in some of Hungary's poorer provincial towns.

Alcoholism may also be a kind of inward expression of political disillusion, or at any rate, a reaction to life in a highly structured society where individuals have relatively little control over their destiny. All the Comecon countries suffer from it, especially the Soviet Union. And in Hungary, it is related not only to the usual health costs and industrial inefficiencies, but

also to a suicide rate that is one of the world's highest. It is the dark side of the Hungarian experience.

The brighter side of the Hungarian experience is also still in evidence, however. Hungarian culture is flourishing, often with massive official support and only rarely against official opposition. It is all a question of interpretation. Article 64 of the constitution declares "the Hungarian People's Republic guarantees freedom of speech, freedom of the press, and freedom of assembly" but adds, judiciously, "in a manner conforming to the interests of socialism and the people." Before 1956, that meant the brutalities of Stalinist socialist realism, and jail or worse for writers or artists who had different ideas. Afterward, the climate slowly thawed. By 1971, the authorities had formally es-

On one of Hungary's isolated farms, or *tanyas*, two women chat while a dog keeps watch over feeding chickens. Nearly 650,000 Hungarians still live on *tanyas*. Although some farmhouses are modernized, most are in poor condition, often lacking even a public water supply.

3

tablished three categories of occupations: the supported, which "raises its voice in support of socialism or human progress"; the tolerated, which "is penetrated by trust in humanity"; and the prohibited, which is "any manifestation of savagery, of ideals imbued with hatred and inhumanity."

In practice, the "tolerated" category is very wide, and writers capable of exercising even a little self-censorship can expect publication and indeed financial success. The dissident writers and artists are far more likely to encounter an endless barrage of small difficulties and inexplicable delays that somehow prevents their work from reaching the public than anything as crude as an outright ban.

The way things are published is important, too. Government statistics, for instance, are generally honestly compiled, and most facts of the nation's economic and social life are a matter of public record, even the unpalatable ones. Thus anyone who wants to spend time in a reference library will find that violent crime in Budapest has been increasing alarmingly since 1970. But if television journalists go so far as to forget their all-important sense of self-censorship and try to present the problem to a mass audience, official fuses will begin to blow and a new subject will have to be found for the program. If the error is repeated too often, these journalists will have to find new jobs.

Censorship is still present, and when the party thinks it necessary the censor does not hesitate to strike. There was a case in 1984, when a junior official of the party-sponsored Writers' Union published a poem in which he described those who had executed Imre Nagy almost 30 years before as "murderers." To the party, this was clearly a "manifestation of savagery," and the poem rapidly found itself in the prohibited category. The poet lost his job and the union was given a shake-up. Other writers got the message; many noted that the Writers' Union had been a little too independent of late and suspected that Kádár had been waiting for just such an opportunity.

Nevertheless, books are published, often privately, with considerable freedom. Moreover, not all of them are of the same uplifting type as *The Spell of the Rail,* a title lauded in the mid-1980s by an official reviewer as "a convincing report on the hard life and harder working conditions of the railroadman, of the oppressive amount of red tape, and of the self-sacrificing devotion and faith of so many of them. . . . The overall impression is of a fine organization, operated by dedicated men."

Hungarians, in fact, are among the world's most prodigious readers, devouring half again as many books, per capita, as the French and twice as many as the Americans. Their general literary intensity is probably encouraged by the unique linguistic isolation imposed upon them by the Magyar tongue, which may also explain why they have never made a major contribution to world literature. Magyar's greatest strength is in its vigorous lyrical poetry, which by its nature is virtually untranslatable, although in its native land it is astonishingly popular.

It is not that Hungarians cannot communicate with outsiders. In the cinema, the most international of artistic media, they have won an enviable critical reputation, and Budapest has a film industry as sophisticated as any in Europe. But then, movie-making has since its inception been in the Hungarian blood: In the hothouse days of early Hollywood, when the world's great film talents jostled each other for success, the Magyar nation contributed a disproportionate share of giants: William Fox (originally Fuchs), founder of 20th-Century Fox; Alexander Korda; director Michael Curtiz; and a constellation of stars ranging from Bela Lugosi and Peter Lorre to Leslie Howard and Tony Curtis. Legend has immortalized an admonitory sign seen on a 1920s studio bulletin board: "It's not enough to be Hungarian. You have to have talent, too."

In the 1980s, the Hungarian cinema has produced several films of unusual sensitivity and moral integrity; its greatest directors, such as Miklós Jancsó, István Szabó and Pál Sándor, have a guaranteed international following, and many Hungarian works have done well in the festival competitions. István Szabó won laurels at the 1981 Cannes Film Festival for his *Mephisto,* the story of an actor caught up in the sinister currents of Hitler's rise in Germany, and received similar acclaim four years later for *Colonel Redl,* an allegory of the corrupting effect of power in the upper echelons of the Hapsburg military establishment.

Although Magyar is by far the most important vehicle for Hungarian culture, it is not the only one. The country includes a number of national minorities, a reminder that however the patchwork of Eastern European political boundaries is stitched, there will always be people separated from their homelands. In Hungary, the non-Magyar elements, which make up 3.4 percent of the total population, are a mixture, in descending numerical order, of Germans, Slovaks, Southern Slavs and Rumanians. Historically,

Swimmers at the Széchényi Baths in Budapest gather to watch a pair of aquatic chess games. Hungary has a strong tradition of chess playing; its national team won the world's first Chess Olympiad in London in 1927.

Hungarians have had a poor record for the treatment of national minorities, oppressing them whenever it was in their power to do so. Today, each minority has a number of important rights enshrined in the constitution, including the right to mother-tongue education up to university level. These rights are respected—most of the people in question are bilingual anyway—and "ethnic" cultural events can usually count on official support.

However, with two other minorities, the Jews and the gypsies, the situation is slightly different. Both groups had suffered dreadfully at the hands of the Germans and the Hungarian fascists during World War II. Yet enough Jews survived to give modern Budapest the largest Jewish community in Eastern Europe, numbering about 75,000 people. They are not recognized as a national minority—most Hungarian Jewish families have been assimilated for many generations—but those who wish to practice their ancestral religion are able to do so freely in Budapest's 30 synogogues and houses of worship. The state provides financial aid for the running of a Jewish hospital and various schools.

A measure of religious tolerance does exist in Hungary, although within limits. The country is about 65 percent Roman Catholic and 30 percent Protestant, and church attendance is high. Relations between the government and the Catholic hierarchy are sometimes a little strained, but ordinary churchgoers practice their faith untroubled by the authorities. In rural areas, the many wayside shrines continue to be as bedecked with flowers as they have been for centuries.

The gypsies are less fortunate, although their very high birthrate assures that there are more than 350,000 of them left. They get few mentions in official publications, no protection as a separate nationality in the constitution and very little sympathy from the Mag-

yar people, who were nomads themselves 1,000 years ago but treat the still-nomadic gypsies at best with condescension and at worst with hostile contempt. In Budapest and a few other cities there exists a highly synthetic gypsy "culture" of Romany bands and persistent violinists serenading tourists at restaurant tables, but the reality of gypsy life is a lot less colorful. Most live in settlements scattered around the fringes of the Great Plain, neither in the socialist economy nor wholly out of it. Here and there a token government project provides low-quality housing for unhappy families living in poverty, but by and large they are treated as an unfortunate historical anomaly that many Hungarians hope will sooner or later simply go away.

The most significant national minority for Hungarians is the one that lives outside Hungary itself. Of the world's 15 million Magyar speakers, approximately one third have their homes beyond the Hungarian frontier. More than four million of them—the living legacy of the Treaty of Trianon more than 60 years ago—are citizens of Hungary's socialist neighbors, and the way they are treated by their host governments goes a long way toward explaining the warmth—or lack of it—of fraternal relationships within the bloc.

The half million in Yugoslavia live in a semiautonomous province, together with Serbs, Croats and various other minorities, with some Magyar education available at university level. For this and other reasons, Hungary has always been as friendly as it dared with the independent Communist state. Rumania, on the other hand, apparently pursued a policy of forced Rumanization of the nearly two million Magyars

in Transylvania, which the country acquired at the end of World War I, lost in 1941 and regained in 1945. Accordingly, Hungary's relations with Rumania are downright icy. The 600,000 in Czechoslovakia—most of them in the former Hungarian domain of Slovakia—are no worse off than the rest of the population. There, relations are polite, if not cordial. But Hungary has to be nice to the Soviet Union, no matter what the Soviets do to the 200,000 Magyars in the Ukraine.

The remaining 1.5 million are distributed throughout the world, from Vienna—which has long been a gathering point for Hungarian émigrés—to faraway Sydney, with the largest Hungarian expatriot community in the United States. Some are exiles from the 1956 revolt, some fled the prewar fascist Horthy regime and some are just wanderers. They seem to thrive on freedom, for the contribution they have made to Western arts and sciences is enormous. In music, there has been Béla Bartók; in philosophy, that protean genius Arthur Koestler; in biology, Leo Szilárd, a Nobel Prize winner; and in mathematics, John von Neumann, also a Nobel Prize winner.

In the mid-1980s, the exiles could—with very few exceptions—return for a visit whenever they wanted. A World Federation of Hungarians exists for their benefit, supported by the state but by no means purely propagandist. Within their small culture, the exiles are a bridge between East and West. It may be that, within the wider world, Hungary, with its pragmatic national economy and the skillful subservience that allows it to live with some real independence under the shadow of its mightiest neighbor, can also serve as a bridge between ideologies. □

Members of the Budapest State Opera House's ballet ensemble rehearse at a daily practice session. Ballets have been held at the Opera House since 1884, and the company, a longtime support of the nation's dance life, has become renowned for both its classical and its modern productions.

A GRACEFUL RELIC OF THE HAPSBURG EMPIRE

Photographs by Hans Wiesenhofer

In 1873, Hungary's capital was given a new identity by the amalgamation of two towns: Buda, the old royal citadel on the hilly west bank of the Danube, and Pest, a commercial center on the flat land across the river. The unification set in motion a hectic process of expansion and urbanization that, in the course of the next 30 years, transformed Budapest from a city of 400,000 people living mostly in single-story buildings into a sophisticated European metropolis of a million inhabitants, with boulevards and avenues emulating those of Paris and Vienna. It became a place of charm and gaiety, where the increasingly prosperous middle classes could enjoy a wealth of amenities, including shops, baths, clubs, hotels and theaters—and continental Europe's first underground railroad. The cafés that sprang up everywhere were thronged all day, their tables, according to a French travel writer of the time, "intruding into the streets, which are alive with the rustling of dresses, laughter and talking."

Today, a century later, Budapest is ringed by prefabricated housing developments, and its two million citizens live under a regime that officially frowns on the bourgeois hedonism of *La Belle Epoque*. Yet it is still possible to find genuine traces of that former golden age. In cafés now run by the state, citizens feast on fine confectionery at marble tables installed a century ago; they can take curative swims in baths decorated in the art nouveau style, which swept Europe in the 1890s, and shop in establishments that have hardly changed their character or appearance since they first opened their doors in the late 19th century.

In Pest's Vörösmarty Square, patrons of the Gerbeaud Café chat in a salon first decorated and furnished in 1884. Its regular customers include descendants of the Hungarian aristocrats who made Swiss confectioner Emil Gerbeaud's coffee shop a favorite haunt of the city's fashionable elite.

Beneath a colored glass roof that has been rolled back to admit the summer air, swimmers exercise in the medicinal waters of the Gellért Hotel's colonnaded pool. Completed in 1918, the baths bloom with the *Jugendstil*, or art nouveau, trend imported from Vienna in the 1880s and 1890s.

A floral art nouveau mosaic medallion adorns the pavement in the entrance to the Gellért pool. Like most of the hotels in central Budapest, the building was damaged during World War II but was restored and modernized in 1945. The Gellért's mosaics were renovated in 1978.

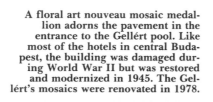

A polished blue light bulb gleams against the white tiles surrounding the swimming pool. The lamps, set into the walls, are modern reproductions in bronze-finished cast iron of the original *Jugendstil* artifacts.

Under the lofty coved ceilings of an elegantly fitted fabric shop that first opened its doors in 1892, a customer deliberates over the choice of dress material. The establishment stocks both costly imported cloth and the products of Hungary's own thriving state-run textile industry.

The treasured glass and china apothecary bottles and jars above, ranked on their white-painted shelves, are of a type that was manufactured in Hungary in the early 19th century. Their graceful flower-garlanded cartouches were a standard form of labeling for vessels of this kind.

An interior of elaborately carved woodwork graces a pharmacy that was established in 1784 and still functions as a modern shop. The carefully preserved fittings, with their multitude of small drawers for pills and lotions, replaced the original interior in the early 19th century.

A mood of leisure and silence broods over the polished columns and high-backed booths of the Apostles Restaurant. Renowned for its dignified

atmosphere since it opened in the early years of the 20th century, the Apostles is a favorite of those seeking traditional Hungarian food and wine.

CZECHOSLOVAKIA'S CAUTIOUS PATH

Early on a Prague morning, citizens cross the Charles Bridge, passing the 30 statues of Christian saints on its parapets. Built in the late 1350s for the Bohemian king Charles IV, the bridge is the oldest of 13 structures that span the Vltava River as it courses through the Czech capital.

Czechoslovakia, like Hungary, has had its attempt at revolution. But unlike Hungary, where soldiers and rebelling citizens fought to the death and blood flowed in the streets of Budapest, Czechoslovakia's efforts to revolutionize socialism were almost entirely peaceful. Yet, decades later, the state was still reverberating from the shock of the attendant upheavals.

In the first eight months of 1968, Czechoslovakia was an exhilarating place to be. The Prague Spring, as it was popularly known, brought winds of change that penetrated even to the innermost sanctum of the ruling Communist party. Activists, both inside and outside the party, were beginning to ask crucial questions about the power of the state and the running of the country. Reformers were campaigning for radical attention to be given to every aspect of government.

As in all other Eastern European countries, the party exercised a rigid control over public life: It ran the government, steered the economy, directed education, monopolized the mass media, censored literature, and it gave out or withheld jobs, privileges and promotions. The senior posts in the government and in industry, communications and education were filled by those whose qualifications for the job included a strong, unswerving loyalty to the party line.

But by late 1967, even some of the party faithful were demanding massive changes. They were deeply dissatisfied with the low morale and economic decline that had set in during the 10-year regime of Antonín Novotný, who was both president of the republic and chief of the Communist party's decision-making Central Committee; they were also calling for an end to censorship, a more flexible approach to the economy and a relaxation of authoritarianism. In the party elections of January 1968, the old guard, orthodox Communists obedient to Moscow, was replaced by a new leadership. Alexander Dubček, a Slovak, became first secretary of the Central Committee of the Czechoslovak Communist party. Ludvík Svoboda, an elder statesman driven out of the government during the Stalinist purges of the early 1950s, replaced Novotný as president.

But the real power resided with Dubček. His unassuming style and comparative liberalism contrasted dramatically with the Stalinist leanings of his predecessor. Novotný had a reputation among his Eastern-bloc allies for being even more of a hard-liner than the Soviets themselves.

On April 5, 1968, the party's Central Committee adopted an official action program that paved the way for sweeping political and economic reforms: The party's hegemony was to be curtailed, and new non-Communist political groups were to be permitted some freedom of action. Individual industries and agricultural enterprises were

4

to have more control over their own programs; the Czechoslovak constitution would be revised; ordinary citizens, in all walks of life, would have more chance to participate in decision making, and would have the right to free speech and free assembly. Communism, in short, would be democratized; Dubček spoke hopefully of "socialism with a human face." The party members who disapproved of these changes held their peace and bided their time.

The atmosphere, especially in the city of Prague, was electric: Artists and writers produced a stream of innovative films, plays and literary works of a sort that would previously have ended up in the censors' waste paper baskets; private citizens were saying things that they would at one time have kept strictly secret. It was not only acceptable but desirable to criticize the status quo.

Encouraged by the presence of a more liberal leadership, the country's writers and journalists became more ambitious, more radical in their attacks on the establishment and more vocal in their demands for change. Hungry for uncensored news and new ideas, the public snapped up Western books and magazines, freely available for the first time since the Communist takeover. Newly outspoken journals, such as *Literární listyi (Literary Gazette)*, were sold out as soon as the issues went on the newsstands. Indeed, few literary reviews in the West could match the Czech journal's weekly circulation of 300,000 copies during the initial exposure of Czech readers to many of the authors who had been officially suppressed for decades.

In June 1968, the journal's editor, Ludvík Vaculík, published a statement entitled *Two Thousand Words to Workers, Farmers, Scientists, Artists and Everyone,* encapsulating the aims of the Prague Spring. His message was simple: The recent reforms, initiated from within the party, were a start, but they did not go nearly far enough. The party, wrote Vaculík, had for too long been in the hands of "power-hungry egotists, reproachful cowards and people with bad consciences." It was time for those who had abused power to be driven from their sinecures by "public criticism, resolutions, demonstrations, a strike or boycott of their doors."

Such concerns were of prime importance to Czechs, particularly to the most highly educated and articulate part of the population. The chief issues for their Slovak neighbors were strikingly different: Slovakians were less worried about civil liberties than about the age-old problem of their own seemingly endless struggle for equal rights and national autonomy. In the general unrest of 1968, these feelings were given new voice. As far as the Slovaks were concerned, the Czechs had always run the country for their own benefit. Slovakia had been ignored or belittled by those in charge for too long. If changes were in the air, the time had come for Slovaks to rise up and demand a better deal for themselves.

Slovak discontent went back to long before the Communist era, to the establishment of the Czechoslovak Republic in 1918. The political marriage between the two neighboring peoples had been an odd one. The Czechs were prosperous, with a thriving industrial economy based on expertise in such areas as light engineering, metallurgy and glassmaking. The Czechs had no doubts about their cultural identity; they knew who they were and where they had come from. The Slovaks, however, entered into the partnership like an orphaned bride without a dowry. For 1,000 years, Slovakia had been merely a forgotten corner of rural Hungary, its population barely in touch with the world beyond the Tatra Mountains and the White Carpathians. The old Hungarian masters had actively suppressed Slovak language and culture and had hardly begun to develop the region economically. Most of the people were poor peasants, languishing in a rural backwater.

At first, the new republic raised Slovak hopes, but the Slovaks soon felt themselves to be as neglected by the Prague government as they had been by Budapest. They experienced a brief but spurious "independence" under Nazi occupation, when the Germans separated Slovakia into an independent puppet regime, but were disappointed when the 1948 Communist takeover brought no sign of full political and economic equality. The Czechs were still in charge.

Despite the new government's efforts to introduce heavy industry, such as the East Slovakian Ironworks in Košice and the Komárno shipyards on the Danube River, the promised development of Slovakia never came to fruition. The highly centralized Prague government was distant and uninterested, and the party hierarchy was overwhelmingly dominated by Czechs in spite of the fact that Slovaks accounted for one third of the state's population. Slovaks were irked, for instance, that only 82 of nearly 600 members of the Czechoslovak diplomatic corps were Slovaks and that half the diplomatic missions sent abroad were composed exclusively of Czechs. It was even murmured, mutinously, that the man wearing the costume of a Slovak shep-

Laundry hangs out to dry from an upper story of a 19th-century tenement in Prague's Malá Strana quarter. Although many of these buildings do not have indoor plumbing, their central location makes them popular in a city that is short of housing.

herd in the Czechoslovak pavilion at the Montreal World's Fair, Expo 67, was in fact a Czech.

During the political ferment of the Prague Spring, some Slovak writers and political activists joined their Czech comrades in the call for democratization. But opinion polls repeatedly indicated that national equality was the No. 1 item on the reform agenda for the vast majority of Slovaks.

No matter how high feelings ran, the 1968 reform debates were not acrimonious, on the whole. Differences between Slovak nationalists and Czechs, or between orthodox Communists and reformers, were aired without violence.

Although the implications of the proposed changes were far reaching, the principal actors in the drama were journalists, intellectuals and politicians. However sympathetic others might be, the bulk of the working population remained interested spectators and did not get involved: There were no national strikes or battles in the streets.

As the Spring movement progressed, some party members, attuned to the temper of their mentors in Moscow, were beginning to quail. At the end of June, the Presidium, the ruling body of the party, issued its own response to Vaculík's inflammatory *Two Thousand Words,* warning that "the political plat-

form on which the declaration is based opens the way for the activation of anti-Communist tendencies and plays into the hands of extremist forces that could provoke chaos and a situation fraught with conflict." Less than eight weeks later, their warnings bore fruit.

At 2300 hours, Central European Time, on the night of August 20, 1968, the inhabitants of Prague heard aircraft flying low over the city—an unaccustomed sound at so late an hour. A Western journalist, enjoying a social evening with his colleagues, remarked that it was probably a tourist charter flight arriving behind schedule from somewhere else in the Eastern bloc.

The journalist very quickly realized his mistake. Throughout the night, units of the 24th Soviet Tactical Air Army moved on Prague's Ruzyně Airport. Elsewhere in the country, Soviet airborne troops took over smaller airports and local landing strips. Four Soviet tank divisions and a division of East Germans sealed the border with West Germany. Five Soviet army divisions and another East German division surrounded the capital. In the meantime, Soviet, Polish, Hungarian and Bulgarian troops occupied the city of Bratislava as well as the remainder of central and western Slovakia, Brno and southern Moravia. All told, half a million Soviet and satellite troops simply took over the country.

Twelve years after the revolution in Hungary, the Soviet Union had again marshaled overwhelming forces to put a stop to a sequence of intolerable events. Official Soviet statements called the reforms a "threat to push the country off the path of socialism." It was said by some witnesses that the young Warsaw Pact soldiers manning the convoys into Prague were shocked to discover just how bitterly the Czechs resented the Soviet presence; they had expected to be greeted as liberators. But resistance was for the most part unarmed and passive: spontaneous demonstrations, distributions of leaflets, broadcasts by a hastily improvised clandestine radio and television service (the necessary electronic skulduggery bore witness to the legendary mechanical genius of the Czechs).

The Soviet Union demanded that the Czechoslovak Communist party repudiate its radical action program, reinstate censorship and put an end to emergent nonparty political activity. Dubček was arrested, spirited to Moscow, held for a short time and released, although he was not dismissed from office until April 1969. Yet he and his fellow reformers were gradually removed from all positions of power in the state and the party, to be replaced by those prepared to adhere more closely to the Soviet line. The process, which the government called "normalization" and dissidents called "repression," had begun. Prague Spring participants and sympathizers were purged from the membership lists of the party, dismissed from their jobs and placed under surveillance.

Virtually overnight, half a million people—party and nonparty members, Marxists and Christians, Maoists and liberals alike—all became "nonpersons." Several thousand historians, teachers, scientists, lawyers, photographers, musicians, novelists, journalists and filmmakers lost their jobs and were transformed, by sheer necessity, into the stokers, taxi drivers, day laborers and window cleaners of Prague. Secret police and government censors were back in business.

But not all the progressive ideas engendered during the Prague Spring were smothered at birth. The Slovaks at long last received the political equality they had fought for. On October 28, 1969, President Ludvík Svoboda signed a federalization bill, altering the constitution and transforming Czechoslovakia into a binational federal state, with Czechs and Slovaks sharing power on an equal basis. Each thus was allowed to form its own legislative body—a Slovak National Council based in Bratislava and a Czech National Council situated in Prague. Representatives from both nations came together in the bicameral federal parliament. Its lower chamber, the House of the People, is divided in proportion to population, with two thirds of its deputies coming from the numerically superior Czech Lands, and the upper chamber, the House of Nations, which is equally divided between Czechs and Slovaks.

The package of federal reforms was accompanied by a massive investment program, designed to bring underdeveloped Slovakia onto an equal economic footing with the Czech Lands. Dubček's successor as party leader, Gustáv Husák was, like Dubček himself, from Slovakia; he had spent more than 10 years in prison during the Stalinist period for his activities on behalf of the Slovak cause. To the dismay of some Czechs, who felt that conditions were not as rosy in the declining industrial areas of Bohemia and Moravia, the lion's share of government spending went to Slovakia.

Since then, new factories have opened, turning out new products such as color televisions for export; older industries, such as coal, steel and engineering, have been modernized and expanded. Roads have been improved and new highways have been built. Employment prospects in the mid-1980s were better than ever before, especially in Bratislava. Before federalization, the 800-year-old Slovak capital had been a decorative but decidedly provincial city, somnolent in comparison to the vibrancy of Prague. As the seat of government for the new Slovak Socialist Republic, Bratislava turned into a boomtown. New office buildings—all massive, squat and bleakly functional in design—stand alongside the ornate 18th-century façade of the old Grassalkovich Palace, whose sculpture-filled halls and gardens accommodate the Slovak headquarters of the national youth movement, the Young Pioneers.

A new highway races past the Gothic turrets and gateways of the Old Town, sending an ever-increasing stream of motor vehicles careering past the door of the magnificent 14th-century Gothic St. Martin's Cathedral.

"It's a wonder they didn't manage to run the road straight through the church itself," acidly remarked one local tour guide. Nevertheless, in federalized Slovakia, a new sense of optimism and confidence has replaced the old provincial diffidence.

Although a substantial share of the annual federal budget has been poured into the economic development of Slovakia, in the mid-1980s, the Czech Lands still accounted for four fifths of the country's industrial production, reflecting their long-established role as centers of trade and technology. Craft industries, such as cutting crystal and glassmaking, have a centuries-old tradition; examples of the Bohemian glass cutter's art graced the court of Emperor Rudolf II in the 1500s; and by the late 19th century, affluent households throughout Europe and America glittered with intricate cut-crystal fruit bowls, decanters, chandeliers and goblets from the Bohemian glassworks of Nový Bor, Železný Brod and Jablonec.

Less decorative, perhaps, but more economically significant, is the Czech industrial heritage. About two thirds of the old Austrian Empire's total industry had plants sited in Bohemia and Moravia, close to rich seams of coal, zinc, nickel and other resources. These plants provided employment for generations of skilled artisans and engineers. After 1918, the industrialists who had flourished under the Hapsburgs helped to build up the economy of the new Czechoslovak Republic.

Tomáš Bat'a, bootmaker to the old imperial army during World War I, turned to the civilian market and soon dominated the world shoemaking industry, exporting his goods even to China. He introduced American-style mechanization to his massive plants in eastern Moravia, along with an unprec-

A fresco of swirling foliage and images of a Czech farmer and a blacksmith decorate a house in Prague's Old Town. The façade was painted by a local artist, Mikoláš Aleš, in 1896.

THE JEWEL ON THE VLTAVA

Throughout the ages, Prague has been celebrated for its beauty. In the hills along the Vltava, the architectural gems of its Romanesque and Gothic past join with legacies of later eras to create a uniquely harmonious whole.

Many of Prague's finest structures date from two crucial periods in its history. In the 14th century, Charles IV beautified the Bohemian capital by adding the Charles Bridge, St. Vitus' Cathedral on Hradčany (Castle Hill) and the beginnings of the New Town, which still contains many fine Gothic buildings. In the 1700s, the inner districts of Prague were transformed by the nation's Hapsburg rulers, who erected a number of magnificent churches and palaces.

As Prague's Old Town Hall clock strikes the hour, life-size wooden statues of the Apostles appear at two small windows set above the dial. Built in 1410, the complex face of the clock records the ascendant zodiacal signs, the movements of the sun and moon, and the date and time.

The ornate bulk of St. Vitus' Cathedral looms behind buildings crowning the ridge of Hradčany. The cathedral, begun in the 1340s by Charles IV and completed only in 1929, displays a variety of styles: A baroque spire caps the Gothic tower, while the twin steeples were added in the 1800s.

In the eastern Bohemian town of Nové Město nad Metují—designated by the state as an architectural monument—three Renaissance houses face the town square. The gables and arcades were added to the original homes when the town was totally reconstructed after a fire in 1526.

edented array of fringe benefits and incentive bonuses for his thousands of workers. By 1930, he employed 6 percent of Czechoslovakia's total labor force. Bat'a's son relocated the business to the West in 1932, but the factory, now owned by the state and renamed Svit, remains one of the world's largest shoe producers.

Another major military contractor to the Hapsburgs, the Škoda Armament Works, founded by the Bohemian engineer and industrialist Emil Škoda in the 1890s, became the largest industrial complex in the young republic. Besides weapons, its forges, workshops and foundries in Pilsen turned out railroad equipment, engines, tools, machinery and automobiles. In the 1920s, the sleek Škodas gliding through the streets of central European cities were prized by the bourgeoisie as status symbols. Today's state-produced Škodas are more utilitarian, but they still earn

export currency, with nearly one third of the 200,000 cars produced annually sold to Czechoslovakia's Eastern trading partners. Another Škoda division has turned its technological talents to the production of atomic reactors for Comecon's emergent nuclear-power industry. And, in a war-torn world, the Škoda armament business continues to thrive: Czechoslovakia is the world's 12th-largest weapons contractor.

The solidity of Czechoslovakia's current industrial base is due at least in part to the fact that it suffered little damage during World War II. The Third Reich had, for safety's sake, moved most of its own industrial activity eastward into Czechoslovakia, on the correct assumption that the country would be less vulnerable to Allied bombing. When the Germans were defeated, Czechoslovakia's industrial infrastructure was still relatively intact.

After the war, the Communist take-

over dramatically, and some observers would maintain disastrously, changed the country's economic landscape. Soviet-style centralized planning dictated the creation of primary industries such as steel; at the same time, traditionally strong sectors, such as light engineering, were starved of investment and allowed to run down.

In an effort to secure formerly westward-looking Czechoslovakia inside the Soviet orbit, the trade flow was deliberately redirected. Until 1948, only 18 percent of Czechoslovakia's exports went to Eastern Europe. The new regime shifted the balance; 74 percent of Czechoslovak trade was with the East by the early 1950s. Encouraged by the Soviet Union, the government turned its back on the old, valuable Western markets. Under Czechoslovakia's first Communist leader, Klement Gottwald and his successor, Antonín Novotný, consumer goods industries, such as Bohemian glass, which had depended on affluent customers in the capitalist West, suffered badly.

Today, the situation is almost the opposite of what it was in the late 1940s, and the U.S.S.R., now Czechoslovakia's biggest single market, accounts for 45 percent of the country's trade. In turn, the Czechs are, along with East Germany, the Soviets' best customers for the crude oil—industry's lifeblood—that flows into Eastern Europe along the Druzhba pipeline. This dependency gives their Soviet partners considerable leverage: In 1968, switching off the flow of oil to Czechoslovakia proved as ominously effective a statement as had the dispatching of Warsaw Pact troops.

After the tremors of 1968, the authorities made strenuous efforts to safeguard the standard of living and to keep the work force placid through wage increases, hefty bonuses and vacations sponsored by the labor unions. Shops were well supplied with basic foodstuffs, as well as luxury items such as cameras, stereo equipment and expensive leather goods to allow people to take advantage of their enhanced spending power. Car ownership in Czechoslovakia increased in a dramatic way. In 1968, there had been one car for every 11.5 citizens of Prague; by 1980, there was one for every 4.8 Praguers, and the figure for the country as a whole was one car per 7.7 inhabitants.

The 1970s were, in a modest way, a boom period: Increased affluence was the reward for political passivity. But in the 1980s, not even state intervention could shield the population from the cold winds blowing through the world economy. The standard of living suffered; prices were rising faster than wages. Both industrial and domestic consumers experienced shortages of essential goods and services. An unobtainable spare part could keep a dozen factory workers idling for days around a shutdown assembly line, or cause an overburdened householder to kick a broken washing machine in despair on discovering that the vital replacement part needed to get it going again might take a year or more to arrive.

But people sought, and found, their own solutions: If they could not manage to get what they wanted through the usual channels, they paid a bribe. At the garage, for example, a generous tip to the mechanic would ensure that a car was ready the following day instead of the week after next. Moreover, it has been observed that no prudent Czechoslovak ever takes a car in to be serviced until every essential component is on the point of collapse; otherwise, any us-

CRUSHING THE PRAGUE SPRING

On August 20, 1968, Czechoslovakia was invaded by 230,000 troops from five Warsaw Pact nations. Led by the U.S.S.R., the forces were to oppose the liberalizing reforms of Communist party leader Alexander Dubček. Dubček was arrested and strategic points in Prague were seized. There was no military resistance, but a wave of demonstrations, sabotage and shootings left 72 citizens dead. Within a week, the occupation army had swelled to almost 500,000, and the so-called Prague Spring was over.

Soviet tanks line a street in central Prague after the invasion of August 1968.

In the snow-clad countryside of Slovakia, a woman trudges home after collecting a basketful of potatoes from the winter storage huts near her village. Although its economy is becoming industrialized, Slovakia still retains its strong agricultural base.

able part would be taken out, sold under the counter on the sly and be replaced in the customer's car by an inferior substitute.

At the butcher's, a small present to the person behind the counter would produce a better cut of meat. The state-employed plumber would answer a call with greater alacrity if it was a "private" job; official customers had to live with their burst pipes a little longer. Money could ensure a place at the university for a marginal candidate: If the university registrar liked good wine, and a parent happened to leave a case in the office, poor exam results may have been overlooked.

Unfortunately, the bribes, clandestine deals and other stratagems that people employed to get what they wanted when they wanted it, all served to exacerbate the original problem. As more goods and services have been siphoned into the country's widespread black economy, delays and shortages in the official sectors have grown increasingly worse.

When goods are impossible to obtain either through official channels or under the counter, an increasing number of citizens are resorting to outright theft. A state-owned toy store in Brno, for example, reported that it had to keep its shopping baskets under lock and key. Customers not only stole the toys, they carried them away in the store's own baskets. State property is regarded as fair game; on a single railroad line in eastern Slovakia, passengers made away with 12,788 pairs of curtains, 4,208 mirrors, and 633 light fixtures in the space of a single six-month period.

Theft and corruption were so widespread in the mid-1980s that the authorities no longer turned a blind eye to these offenses and pretended that such things could not possibly happen in a workers' state. An economist, writing in one of the government-sponsored weeklies, commented with some bemusement that "theft from the state is committed increasingly by people who display no other signs of maladjustment and cannot be described as antisocialist elements. . . . The perpetrators are an unusually motley group, ranging from recidivists loath to do an honest day's work to university-educated people with unblemished civic and work records."

Milan Šimečka, a Czechoslovakian dissident, is intrigued by the way his compatriots play the system. The country is full of contradictions, for which even the natives can find no logical explanation: "Cafés, pubs and restaurants are packed the whole day long, although everyone has a job to go to. The mountains are thronged with skiers whose equipment has cost more than half an average annual salary. Almost all young people are informed about the productions of rock groups whose recordings have never been broadcast by Czechoslovak radio. In the country with the most expensive gasoline, the streets are packed every morning with cars driven by people hurrying to work."

Helped, no doubt, by their skillful use of the black economy, most Czechs live comfortably enough, even in periods of low wages, shortages and general financial gloom. In comparison with many of their Eastern-bloc neighbors, they are, in any case, reasonably well off. Only the East Germans are richer; the Poles, Rumanians and Bulgarians are far poorer.

The Czechoslovaks are a fairly well-nourished people, and they earn for-

eign currency by exporting such food products as hops for beer making, hams and sausages, pickles and fruit preserves. This is achieved despite the fact that farming accounts for a smaller share of produced national income than anywhere else in Eastern Europe: 12 percent of the work force is employed in agriculture, and virtually all farms are collectivized. Food stores are adequately stocked and lines—an inevitable fact of life for customers elsewhere in Eastern Europe—comparatively rare. Restaurants are filled by natives as well as by foreign visitors, and most of the items offered on the menu actually appear to be available—something taken for granted elsewhere in

the world, perhaps, but not, say veteran travelers, in Eastern Europe. In the larger towns, bakeries tempt the eye and menace the waistline with rococo pastry confections that are as much a reminder of Hapsburg rule as the beswagged and gilt-encrusted Church of St. Nicholas in Prague's Old Town.

At home, Czechs and Slovaks are pork-and-dumpling eaters, varying their diet on festive occasions with carp from the thousands of fishponds that dot southern Bohemia. These were created by nobles and bishops five centuries ago to provide Lenten fare in their landlocked domains. Meals are washed down with copious draughts of good Bohemian beer—particularly in the

Czech Lands; but this is less so in wine-growing Slovakia.

The pale golden, light-bodied beer brewed in Pilsen is celebrated throughout Europe. Although Czechoslovakian beer earns a considerable amount of export currency, only 10 percent leaves the country. The rest is quaffed enthusiastically by the residents, who are among the thirstiest beer drinkers in the world: Every inhabitant consumes, in statistical terms if not in fact, 40 gallons annually.

Alcoholism is a subject of increasing state concern and the cause of much absenteeism in the workplace. In an attempt to combat this serious and widespread problem, ubiquitous posters

warn citizens that the consumption of alcohol endangers their health. Stringent penalties are meted out to drunk drivers, who are relieved of their operator's licenses at the first offense; there is no right of appeal.

To a Western visitor, Prague, with its traffic jams, looks as bustling—and sounds as cacophonous—as any city back home. The Škodas and East German Wartburgs that choke the city's narrow medieval streets are not known for their low pollution emission. Their exhaust fumes combine with the dust and smoke released from domestic and factory chimneys to produce a dense chemical haze.

Prague is overwhelmingly a coal-burning city; 90 percent of the capital's energy is provided by lignite, the crumbly brown coal mined from the seams at Sokolov and elsewhere in Bohemia. Lignite is not the cleanest of fuels, and it emits large quantities of sulfur dioxide fumes when it is burned. In one five-year period in the 1980s, it was estimated that more than 250,000 tons of sulfur dioxides, carbon monoxides and nitrogen dioxides were released into the atmosphere.

Outside the urban centers, the country's blighted environment points to more unmonitored industrial activity. When pollution became a subject of international concern during the 1960s, conventional Communist wisdom dismissed it as an exclusively capitalist disease. Profit-hungry Western factories spewed out filth untrammeled; socialist factory smokestacks were, it seemed, exempt. Polluted rivers in Eastern-bloc countries soon proved this assumption wrong, however: Managers of state industries, keen to fulfill production quotas, were as

Once-healthy conifers in northwestern Czechoslovakia stand stricken by acid rain. Industrial pollution has brought widespread ecological disaster to the nation's woodlands: More than 20 percent have been either killed or irrevocably damaged.

guilty as their profit-motivated colleagues elsewhere.

In 1983, the Czechoslovak Academy of Sciences drew up a report whose findings were so devastating that they were withheld from publication. Dissidents who had access to the document leaked it to the West. The text makes grim reading: "The whole ecological balance has been upset." The report states that, because of increasing levels of pollution, 30 percent of Czechoslovakia's fish, 60 percent of its amphibians, 30 percent of its reptiles and 35 percent of all mammals are now endangered, and the butterfly population has decreased by 80 percent.

Trees and other plant life are also in peril. By the year 2000, it is estimated that 60 percent of the formerly lush forests of Bohemia and Moravia will be either beyond saving or completely destroyed by pollution. Sulfur dioxide-bearing acid rain, which is a threat to the trees of Europe, has no recognition of East-West political boundaries.

Water pollution is another concern. Between 1976 and 1980, the amount of unpurified sewage in municipal water supplies increased by 64 percent. It is estimated that the equivalent of almost one billion American dollars would be necessary to clean up the water in the capital alone. The Communist party's daily Czech newspaper, Rudéprávo, acknowledged that more than 90 percent of the water supply had to be chemically treated to make it safe for human consumption. This is not, to be sure, a problem that is confined to Eastern Europe.

In the north Bohemian coal-mining districts, the polluted air has so endangered children's health that the state gives grants enabling whole communities to send their children away to the

A tractor plowing a field at Mělník, north of Prague, is dwarfed by a modern coal-burning power station. Sixty percent of Czechoslovakia's immense energy consumption is fed by coal, mostly low-grade lignite mined from seams in north Bohemia.

A CHRONOLOGY OF KEY EVENTS

400-600 A.D. Slav migrants colonize the area of present-day Czechoslovakia. One tribe known as Czechy (Czechs) settles in the regions of Bohemia and Moravia; Slovak Slavs occupy Pannonia.

c.830 The Great Moravian Empire, a loose confederation of Slav peoples, stretches from Bohemia across Slovakia to western Hungary and Poland.

863 Byzantine missionaries Cyril and Methodius arrive to convert the Moravian Empire to Christianity.

c.906 Magyars from Hungary destroy the Moravian Empire and capture Slovakia, which will remain a Hungarian possession for the next 1,000 years.

895-1306 Bohemia and Moravia are ruled by Czech Přemyslid princes from their capital, Prague. The Bohemian kingdom reaches the height of its power under Přemysl Otakar II, extending from the Oder River to the Adriatic coast.

c.1000 German traders and artisans settle in Bohemia.

1346-1378 During the brilliant reign of Charles IV, the arts and sciences flourish in Bohemia. Prague's university, the first in central Europe, is founded in 1348.

1390-1415 Czech religious reformer Jan Hus preaches against papal power and corruption, until he is found guilty of heresy and burned at the stake.

1419 Rebellious followers of Hus—known as Hussites—throw pro-papal councilors from the upper windows of the New Town Hall *(below);* this "First Defe-

nestration of Prague" provokes the 15-year-long Hussite Wars.

1526 The election of Ferdinand I of Austria to the Bohemian throne brings Bohemia into the tight orbit of Hapsburg rule for the next 382 years.

1618 Czech Protestant nobles hurl two Hapsburg representatives out of an upper window in Prague Castle; this Second Defenestration sparks an uprising that leads to the wider European conflict of the Thirty Years' War.

1620 Hapsburg troops under the deposed Bohemian king, Ferdinand II, defeat the Czech armies at the Battle of the White Mountain near Prague. Protestantism is proscribed in Bohemia, and some 300,000 Czechs emigrate.

1749 German is made the official language of Bohemia.

1781 Under the relatively enlightened Austrian emperor, Joseph II, serfdom is abolished and freedom of worship is granted in Bohemia.

1848 A pan-Slav congress in Prague agitates for political reform; in the same year, Czech Jews receive full civil and political rights.

1878 Inspired by nationalist sentiments and the Bohemian folk tradition, *The Slavonic Dances,* written by Czech composer Antonín Dvořák, are performed for the first time in Prague.

1915-1916 Nationalist leader Tomáš Masaryk flees to Paris where he and Eduard Beneš form the Czechoslovak National Council, which becomes the nucleus of a future Czechoslovak government.

1918 With the destruction of the Austro-Hungarian Empire after World War I, the independent Republic of Czechoslovakia is proclaimed on October 28. Tomáš Masaryk is elected to serve as the new state's first president.

1921 The Czech author Jaroslav Hašek writes the first part of the satirical work *The Good Soldier Švejk (right).*

1924 Franz Kafka, the 30-year-old Prague-born Jewish author, dies of tuberculosis. His major novels *The Trial* and *The Castle,* written in German, express 20th-century alienation and anxiety.

1938 The Munich Agreement, signed by England, France, Germany and Italy, forces Czechoslovakia to cede the Sudetenland to Germany; land given to Poland

and Hungary reduces the country's area and population by a third.

1939 Czechoslovakia is occupied by Nazi troops.

1945 Prague is liberated by Soviet troops. Beneš returns from exile to form a coalition government with the Communists.

1946 In the first and last postwar free election, the Communists win 35 percent of the total vote; two years later, the Communists seize control of the government in a bloodless coup.

1951-1953 Political purges and show trials suppress opposition to the regime.

1968 The more liberal style of rule introduced by Communist party leader Alexander Dubček results in the invasion of Czechoslovakia by Warsaw Pact troops to restore Soviet hegemony; Dubček is later succeeded by hard-liner Gustáv Husák.

1969 On January 1, Czechoslovakia becomes a federal state composed of the Czech Socialist Republic and the Slovak Socialist Republic. On January 16, a Prague University student, Jan Palach, sets himself on fire as an act of protest against censorship.

1977-1981 *Charter '77,* a manifesto signed by 1,000 Czech citizens, criticizes the Czech government for acting in violation of the 1975 Helsinki Agreement that guarantees human rights. Between 1979 and 1981, many of the signatories are tried and sent to prison.

1984 Government authorities rule that the Jazz Section of the Musicians' Union is illegal.

1987 Two leaders of the Jazz Section are convicted and jailed for unauthorized distribution of newsletters. Party leader Gustáv Husák, under Soviet pressure, speaks of the need for economic and social "reform."

mountains for a taste of cleaner air.

"People become ill frequently as a result of the polluted water and air," observed a Czech scientist who has lived for a decade in north Bohemia. "If you go to the doctor with a sore throat, a cough or a headache, the GP will refuse to acknowledge it as an illness and will tell you, 'You must have opened a window last night. Don't worry, it will go away in a few days. Just keep your windows closed.' "

In response to the crisis, the government has passed a battery of antipollution laws. But, as in the West, economic pressures often take precedence over environmental concerns. Factory managers habitually flout the law. They complain, as do their capitalist counterparts elsewhere, that adherence to antipollution regulations slows down production and imposes unacceptable costs. The government, in common with many governments elsewhere in the world, is less inclined to be swayed by such arguments when faced with looming environmental disaster. Although some critics might condemn government intervention as "too little, too late," officials have tried to provide an improved transit system for Prague to combat the ill effects of too many vehicles, greater vigilance over industrial pollution and experiments on the development of "emission resistant" species of trees to replace those already doomed by acid rain.

European environmentalists are concerned that such measures may be too late to stop the rot. But it is clear that the country's increasingly fragile ecosystem will only survive if the state makes its protection a higher priority. Czechoslovakia has no Western-style environmental pressure groups to blow the whistle on industrial polluters and badger the authorities on conservation issues. The butterflies are at the mercy of the bureaucrats.

The political climate in present-day Czechoslovakia does not encourage independent pressure groups, whatever their cause or campaign. However, it is also fair to say that the great majority of Czechoslovaks are not characteristically political activists. One of their own compatriots, an émigré political scientist, has described them as "a nation of little men . . . fond of their privacy, their families, proud of their occupational skills."

The children are the most politically mobilized sector of the community. Membership in the party's youth organizations—the Young Pioneers for six- to 15-year-olds and the Socialist Union of Youth for older teenagers—unlocks the door to a vast range of recreational activities: free summer camps, sports facilities, hobby clubs and excursions. The younger generation also provides an immediately available and enthusiastic public for events of state; when necessary, whole schools are called out to line the streets, to cheer and wave flags at whatever visiting dignitaries are passing through.

Among the older generation, those who are ambitious, professionally or politically, opt for party membership; about 11 percent of the population carry party cards. Most of them will turn out regularly and dutifully for their fair share of mass meetings, rallies, voluntary work projects and congresses of the state-run Revolutionary Labor Union Movement.

Zealous political activism is mainly the preserve of those who wish to rise high in the Communist hierarchy. Czechoslovakia, like its allies, has its own party elite, whose political rank buys the same sorts of privileges that personal wealth buys in the West. Since 1968, its members have kept a relatively low profile: Little is known about their personalities or their private lives.

Nevertheless, Czechoslovakia is a fairly egalitarian society, with a relatively narrow gap between the living standards of its richest and poorest members. This balance is not purely the result of socialism. Centuries of Austrian rule over the Czech Lands, and Hungarian domination of Slovakia, eclipsed any native aristocracy. The Czechs were mostly industrial workers, artisans or middle-class professionals and entrepreneurs; the Slovaks were peasant farmers. Tensions between the two nationalities still remain, but neither community has a heritage of ingrained class prejudices, and social groups in both are open and fluid, and without the status-seeking and snobbery endemic in more stratified societies. In a country where virtually everyone is a public employee, the old master-servant relationship is absent. Some people may be able to advance further in their careers than others, but there is a widespread appreciation that everyone is working for the same boss: the state.

Milan Šimečka has observed that this egalitarianism "gives one a comforting feeling of belonging. You cannot tell 'who's who' in the street, the café, the pub or the restaurant. Nor can you tell by the cars people drive."

On weekends, Czechoslovakia's city dwellers point their Škodas or bicycles toward the countryside to indulge in a favorite national pastime: the country weekend. The rural areas, particularly in the scenic, heavily forested region of southern Bohemia, are easily accessible from Prague and are dotted with privately owned weekend cottages. Some are old farmhouses that have remained in the same family for generations, but the vast majority are tiny dwellings, A-frame huts with fairly primitive amenities, on patches of ground that are leased from the state at nominal rents. Many are painstakingly hand built by their proprietors, often from prefabricated kits and sometimes with state-owned tools and materials discreetly acquired through the black economy.

Once the roof is in place and the tiny porch is painted, the occupants pass their leisure hours in the pursuit of country pleasures: pickling cucumbers in the summer, making jam, gathering and drying wild mushrooms, or simply sitting on their front steps drinking beer and gossiping with the neighbors. If they choose to watch television, they will generally tune to an Austrian station, whose capitalist programing is far more popular than the lackluster state productions. Unperturbed by this electronic access to the West, the authorities in some districts have erected communal aerials to help residents pick up Austrian broadcasts.

City dwellers are energetic concert-goers. Old Hapsburg palaces still resound with the symphonic masterpieces and chamber suites composed under the patronage of their former occupants. Thousands of professional and amateur orchestras and smaller ensembles perform throughout the country to audiences numbering in the millions. The country's musical heritage is not only the staff of cultural life, but a solid source of foreign currency: During the past two decades, Czechoslovakia has exported more than 40 million records, more than two thirds of them classical.

Soccer is a national passion, with

The pride of Czechoslovakia's 1,748 state-controlled farms—and the most successful advertisement for its mainly collectivized agriculture—is the Slušovice Cooperative Farm. Situated in the Gottwaldov region of central Moravia, the cooperative was founded in 1949 when the village of Slušovice began to cultivate its fields collectively. Today, the cooperative encompasses 17 villages and 15,120 acres of arable land—more than twice the size of most Czech farming co-ops. With its get-ahead, entrepreneurial philosophy, the enterprise is a symbol of achievement in all aspects of modern agribusiness.

Although its primary concern remains agriculture—it produces mainly beef and milk but also wheat, corn and barley—the co-op has rapidly branched into more lucrative avenues. These include the manufacture of farm machinery, fertilizer and pesticides, a biochemical division working with animal feed, and a civil-engineering unit building shops and housing.

This range of activities employs a work force of 3,000 who, with their families, enjoy benefits that include free health-care facilities, schools, and entertainment and sports centers, including a race-course. As in all collectives, wages are set by the state; the cooperative's highest earners are the truck drivers. However, those in top management are given company cars. Slušovice's chairman gets a BMW, general managers use Renaults, and unit managers the locally made Škoda.

The director of Slušovice' s Agricultural Unit—the largest of the co-op's six divisions—relaxes at home with his family. A graduate of Prague University, he has spent a number of years as an agronomist in the region.

A road sign carrying the name of Czechoslovakia's biggest cooperative farm stands outside one of the collective's 17 member villages. All participating communities receive practical aid and funding from the Slušovice project for constructing shopping centers and other amenities.

At a weekly board meeting, Slušovice's chairman and managers address section heads. Senior managers receive roughly the same salary as manual workers, and the chairman's pay is not always the highest.

On a misty morning *(left)*, jockeys from Slušovice compete in an off-season practice run at the cooperative's racetrack, opened in 1981. Slušovice owns 55 racehorses and keeps 40 mares for breeding.

Workers from the Agricultural Unit take a short break from cutting grass grown to feed the 2,000 head of cattle on the cooperative's farms. Only 10 percent of Slušovice's income derives from agriculture: Surplus produce and livestock are exported to Italy, Austria and Eastern-bloc states.

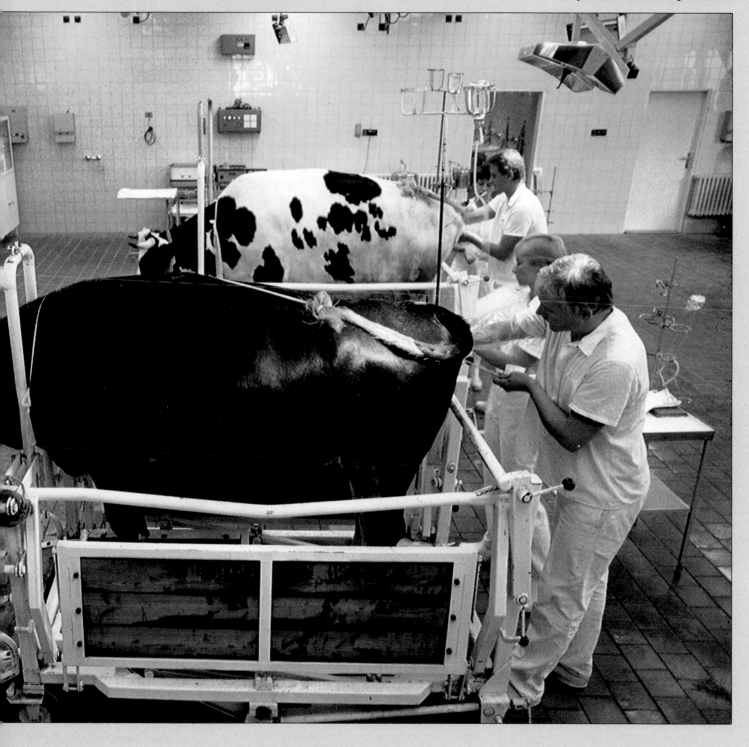

Superstar Ivan Lendl follows through on his serve during the 1985 U.S. Open tennis tournament at Flushing Meadow, in Queens, New York, which he won. Czechs take sports seriously; all children participate, and future champions are groomed in the country's 17 sports schools.

more than half a million players registered in teams and local clubs. Ice hockey, however, threatens to overtake it as the country's favorite spectator sport. Formidable in their helmets and protective padding, the teams who slam their pucks across the ice in the stadiums at Prague or Bratislava are world champions of long standing. When the national squads compete against their archrivals from the U.S.S.R., ordinary life comes to a virtual standstill until the results of the games are known, sending whole communities into mass celebrations or deep despondency.

Not all sports are so aggressive. In a country with some of the most ravishing mountain scenery in central Europe, it is not surprising that hiking, climbing and skiing are popular.

But the sport that fires the blood and excites the ambitions of the country's youth is without a doubt tennis. Since the 1940s, Czechoslovakia has produced a galaxy of international tennis stars, among them Jaroslav Drobný, Jan Kodeš, Hana Mandlíková and Ivan Lendl. The more purist of Czechoslovakia's allies have sometimes dismissed Czech success at the highly individualistic sport of tennis as a throwback to the nation's bourgeois past, but even Moscow is now importing Czechoslovakian tennis coaches to nurture its own budding talents.

Every town has its well-tended public courts and tennis clubs, with young hopefuls starting on the road to Wimbledon as early as seven or eight years of age. They are zealously coached, tested and nursed through a highly organized tournament program, where talent scouts single out the best of the contestants for further training at one of the country's 17 special sports schools. Here, conventional education

is sandwiched into a grueling schedule of tennis training.

The hard work is worth the effort: Professional success brings fame, fast cars, foreign travel, hard currency and a glamorous lifestyle. In return, the government asks only that international tennis stars give 20 percent of their hefty earnings back to the state. It is in the national interest to keep these celebrities happy, lest they follow the example of world champion Martina Navrátilová, who defected to the United States in 1975.

Today, defections are relatively uncommon. In the period immediately after August 1968, however, an indeterminate number of Czechs and Slovaks who were traveling in the West chose to extend their holidays indefinitely; they

were joined subsequently by an estimated 100,000 or more of their compatriots. Between 1981 and 1986, about 3,500 Czechs managed to move to the West each year. A very small minority achieved this through legal channels: The dissident novelists Josef Škvorecký and Milan Kundera, for instance, departed with the blessings of the authorities, who were glad to be rid of such articulate gadflies. Others got out illicitly by traveling to Yugoslavia, still a socialist country although not a member of the Soviet bloc. Once they made it that far, crossing the border to the West was relatively easy.

At home, most people have adjusted to, or resigned themselves to, an apolitical life. But the dreams of the Prague Spring have not been totally forgotten, and dissent flows like an underground river through the society.

Once in a while, the stream rises to the surface. In 1977, a group of 1,000 writers, academics and other concerned citizens put their names to a charter petitioning the government to adhere to the tenets of the United Nations Covenant on Human Rights (and of Czechoslovakia's own constitution); they asked for more political freedom, relaxation of censorship and an end to the systematic persecution of those dissidents who had been active during and after the Prague Spring.

Charter '77 was a bold gesture that cost many of its signatories their jobs— and, in several cases, their liberty. But the activists of *Charter '77* and its offspring, VONS—the Committee to Defend the Unjustly Prosecuted—continue to publish, however sporadically, unofficial documents that discuss the state of the economy, the environment, health and social services, and the arts. These unofficial—and therefore ille-

At the end of an antique car rally in east Bohemia, where entries are mostly interwar Czech Pragas and Tatras, an owner fixes badges to his elegant vehicle. Collecting and restoring old cars is a national passion; the country has 45 antique-auto clubs.

gal—publications are known, as they are in the equally censor-ridden Soviet Union, by the Russian name of *samizdat*.

For a growing number of Czechs and Slovaks, religion provides a context for opposition. Unlike their counterparts in Poland or Hungary, where the Communist state has worked out some form of accommodation with the established churches, the Czechoslovak authorities were, for a long time, relentless in their persecution of believers. In the 1950s, the ruling Stalinists closed monasteries and seminaries, imprisoned priests, and brought the Catholic and Protestant churches under the direct control of the state. Never going as far as to ban religious worship, they made sure that

the only clergy allowed in the pulpits were those sympathetic—or at least obedient—to the regime.

A brief thaw occurred in the 1960s; but after August 1968, more than 500 Catholic priests and Protestant pastors were suspended from duty, and the state once more tightened restrictions on all Church activities, controlling the jobs and salaries of clerics. Churchgoers, while not overtly persecuted, are well aware that too much visible piety may have a damaging effect on their career prospects.

About two thirds of the population is, at least nominally, Catholic, with the greatest concentration of communicants in Slovakia. In the late 1970s, Slo-

vak Catholics spearheaded the formation of an unofficial, totally unauthorized religious committee, essentially a second, "secret" Catholic Church. Operating without a formal religious hierarchy, without access to state funds, without buildings or official representatives, this alternative underground movement has attracted a growing membership. Dissident priests, suspended from their jobs in the state-supervised official Church, say Mass and perform the sacraments in private houses.

Protestants, too, have formed their clandestine congregations. A thriving underground religious publishing network turns out a growing number of

4

Bibles, prayer books, hymnals and theological *samizdat*. At least 100 regularly issued journals, newspapers, magazines and bulletins on religious topics appear for sale on either a weekly or a monthly basis.

Despite a barrage of official obstacles and harassment, publishers of secular *samizdat* are equally energetic. The dissident journalists, novelists and political commentators who came into the open (and lost their jobs) during the Prague Spring and after *Charter '77* have continued to write. They do not submit their manuscripts to the state-run publishing houses, which would turn them down for political reasons (even if the offical excuse was some literary complaint over structure and style). Instead, these writers turn to unofficial and technically illegal independent publishing houses such as the Padlock Press, which was founded by Ludvík Vaculík, author of the *Two Thousand Words* that so alarmed the authorities in 1968.

With no access to the printing presses and binding machinery controlled by the state, Padlock Press publications are typed with multiple carbons instead of being printed, and are hand-stapled or glued instead of bound. Vaculík relies on a large pool of trustworthy volunteer typists. But typewriters themselves are often hard to come by. In Czechoslovakia, each machine has to be individually registered and licensed by the authorities. Distribution, too, is a problem: No official bookstore or newsstand will touch these publications. Instead, they are circulated clandestinely, passed from hand to hand by trusted friends and colleagues.

Despite these practical difficulties, coupled with frequent police raids, confiscations of manuscripts, deten-

tions and interrogations, Vaculík has managed to publish hundreds of works of poetry, history, literary criticism, philosophy and sociology, which are discreetly conveyed to all parts of Czechoslovakia and across the border into the West.

Uncensored music worries the authorities as much as uncensored literature. After 1948, all forms of Western popular music, from New Orleans blues to slick Broadway numbers, were banned by the Communist regime.

This was not the first time the censors had suppressed popular music. During the Nazi occupation, the Germans forbade the playing of the "degenerate" American jazz passionately admired by Czech youth. After the war, during the repressive years under the Stalinist regime, new musical influences continued to find ways of slipping across the border; and by the 1960s, there was a proliferation of folk, rock and jazz bands throughout the country.

In the nervous aftermath of the Prague Spring, government officials again began to listen to the music; they disliked what they heard. Once more, many groups were denied the right to perform in public because of their allegedly "negative social effect." And musicians are still banned from public performance, sometimes even jailed, for offenses ranging from overlong hair to subversive lyrics.

For many of these artists and their audiences, music and politics are inextricably intertwined. During the 1970s and early 1980s, the Jazz Section of the Musicians' Union became a focus for dissident culture, sponsoring seminars, arts festivals and publications that went far beyond musical subjects to explore environmental issues, radical theater and alternative interpretations of

Czechoslovak history. The Jazz Section's official membership list never rose above the state-imposed limit of 3,000, but copies of its literature managed to find their way into the hands of an estimated 100,000 readers, including the teen-age children of some high-ranking party officials.

The government launched a campaign of official harassment, which culminated in the cancellation of an international jazz festival in Prague in 1982, only hours before it was due to open. Thousands of disappointed ticket holders and hundreds of foreign guest-performers were left angrily milling in the streets. A heavy police presence prevented a riot; but within a few hours, the walls of the Czech Ministry of Culture had been sprayed with graffiti proclaiming: "We shall not let you kill the Jazz Section!"

But kill it they did. A barrage of attacks on the Jazz Section in the state-controlled press was followed by a hefty bill presented to the organizers for hitherto unrequested "back taxes." The parent Musicians' Union refused subtle and not-so-subtle government requests to disband its contentious offspring. Then, in 1984, the state dissolved the entire Musicians' Union, Jazz Section and all.

Despite—some observers would say because of—these pressures, a dissident culture survives. People cluster discreetly in Prague apartments to watch private performances by underground theater groups; dog-eared carbon copies of unauthorized novels pass from hand to hand; young people gather in barns, orchards and obscure suburban dance halls to listen to banned musicians or to sing the songs of such rock groups as the Plastic People of the Universe, who were imprisoned in the

period of "normalization" that followed the Prague Spring.

They are afraid of the old for their memory,
They are afraid of the young for their in-
nocence . . .
They are afraid of art,
They are afraid of books and poems,
They are afraid of records and tapes . . .
They are afraid of Democracy . . .
They are afraid of Socialism . . .
So why the hell are we afraid of Them?

A member of the Plastic People band, in a *samizdat*, offers an explanation for the growth of this counterculture, linking such disparate elements as dissident economists and jazz saxophonists, revisionist historians and radical acrobats: "This unorganized community of people would never have come into being had not the pressure from the establishment been so unbearable."

A whole new generation has grown up since Czechoslovakia's Warsaw Pact allies sent their tanks into Prague to put an end to what they saw as dangerous deviations from the party line. The memory of that brutal act lingers, but life inevitably moves on. The reorganization of the state into a federation of two internally autonomous socialist republics, the Czech and the Slovak, has alleviated simmering resentments and fundamental inequalities that have existed since the founding of Czechoslovakia. At a time when socialist neighbors such as Hungary are becoming increasingly innovative, the return to a conservative, authoritarian version of Communism has created new stresses and schisms between those who prefer to keep their heads down and live quietly and those who feel impelled, whatever the pitfalls might be, to challenge the power of the state. ☐

In the east Slovakian mountain resort of Ždiar, mourners in a funeral procession follow a horse-drawn coffin through the snow to the cemetery. Behind them stand the brightly painted wooden homes of local farmers, who often rent out rooms to tourists visiting the village.

ON THE ROAD
TO THE BLACK MADONNA

Photographs by Christopher Pillitz

For the devoutly Catholic population of Poland, the zenith of the religious year comes every August, at the Feast of the Assumption of the Virgin Mary. Under the blazing summer sun, hundreds of thousands of pilgrims make their way on foot toward the nation's holiest shrine, the monastery of Jasna Góra—"The Hill of Light"— in the southern town of Czstochowa. Proceeding at a solemn pace, the marchers take nine days to cover the 172 miles from Warsaw; and all along the route, new streams of the faithful converge to swell the numbers. The object of their devotion is the Black Madonna, a Byzantine icon darkened—apparently—with age, enshrined within one of Jasna Góra's chapels.

The portrait is revered for its miraculous powers. In 1656, when Poland was rent by invading armies, the monastery was besieged by Swedish troops. Legend tells that the enemy's cannonballs bounced harmlessly off the walls; and when the Madonna's image mysteriously appeared, hovering above the fray, the invaders fled in terror. A grateful King Jan Kazimierz named the Virgin "Queen of Poland," extolling her as the nation's savior.

Early in the next century, when the miracle was still within living memory, the pious began to flock to Częstochowa for the Virgin's feast, the first in a long line of pilgrimages winding through the generations. For many of today's marchers, participation is as much a political statement as a declaration of faith, and the music that urges them on their way includes protest songs from the banned labor union movement, Solidarity, as well as traditional hymns of praise from the ancient liturgy.

Anticipating the arrival of pilgrims bound for Czstochowa, villagers stand ready with cold water to refresh the marchers. In farms and villages along the route, the offering of food and drink is an annual ritual—and the affirmation of a shared faith.

A day in August on the road to Jasna Góra sees the pilgrims strolling through farmland, with priests, nuns and nurses among the leaders, setting the pace in the summer heat. With up to 25 miles to cover before nightfall, everyone has been on the move since just after sunrise. They pause briefly for a hasty meal of steaming soup from one of the field kitchens or a snack offered by villagers along the route. During the break in the journey, the nurses, who treat sprains and blistered feet, take time to join in a special mass held in their honor.

At night, people find shelter where they can. The elderly bed down in churches or in the homes of local families; the young pitch tents in the open fields and end the day with songs around the campfire.

On the eve of their arrival at Częstochowa, the 40,000-strong contingent of pilgrims from Warsaw gathers for Mass on a riverbank near the village of Mstów. With arms upraised, they join in a song for peace, led by their parish priests.

At the end of their arduous journey, devout pilgrims kneel in prayer before the Black Madonna. Normally concealed behind a screen, the icon on this occasion is unveiled to the worshippers in a ceremony heralded by a trumpet's blast.

From a mounting of gilt embroidery, the Virgin gazes down on a mass conducted by a priest assisted by acolytes in the somber chapel. The painting is believed to be of Byzantine origin, dating back to the year 500; it reached its present site, by unknown means, in the 14th century.

POLAND: A NATION IN TORMENT

On a small private farm west of Warsaw, a farmer takes a break from plowing. The private farms, which occupy 77 percent of agricultural land in Poland, produce greater yields per acre than the state sector, despite the fact that they receive much less investment aid.

In August 1980, Poland hit the headlines as no other Eastern European country had done since the Prague Spring. What put it there was the extraordinary strike in the Baltic Sea port of Gdańsk, which gave birth to the first independent labor union ever recognized by a Soviet-bloc state: "NSZZ 'Solidarność,' " as the Polish workers christened it, the "Independent Self-Governing Labor Union 'Solidarity.' " For 15 and a half heady months, pictures of Poland and of the face of a previously unknown electrician from the Lenin Shipyard in Gdańsk, Lech Wałęsa—became familiar to television viewers and readers of print media throughout the Western world.

But on December 13, 1981, claiming that the 10-million-strong democratic movement was bringing Poland to the verge of anarchy, the country's authorities put an abrupt and violent end to Solidarity's officially recognized existence. General Jaruzelski declared a "state of war." After the clampdown, Poland remained in the limelight. But the scenes that appeared again and again on Western television screens were now images of repression: police armed with water cannon and tear gas charging crowds of young Solidarity demonstrators or, more poignantly still, dispersing groups of old women gathered around a cross of flowers in front of a church, defiantly singing patriotic hymns and raising two fingers in the V-for-Victory sign, as the water cannon scattered the blossoms.

The Polish tradition of resistance to an alien state authority is a long one. It goes back at least two centuries, to the time of the partitions. The revolt against Russian rule launched in Kraków in 1794 by the patriotic General Tadeusz Kościuszko, uniting nobles and peasants, Christians and Jews, country and city dwellers, was the first in what has been a long series of national uprisings and insurrections.

Many young people in Poland today, engaged in printing and distributing underground publications and involved in other unofficial opposition activities, are well aware of this tradition. They place themselves in the direct line of succession from Kościuszko through the Warsaw Uprising of 1944 to the leaders of Solidarity. And these young Poles would probably also affirm that they are fighting essentially the same enemy as their predecessors: directly, the Russian Empire, and more broadly, the geopolitical agreements between the great European powers that, most recently at Yalta in 1945, sacrificed Poland's freedom and independence to their own security interests.

This powerful sense of tradition helps make Poland one of the most proudly recalcitrant and consistently contrary nations in the whole Soviet bloc. But the version of the recent past it implies is simplified and abbreviated; it is as much mythology as history.

It is true that Poland would never

135

5

freely have chosen Soviet socialism as its form of government in 1945. Stalin himself said that introducing Communism to Poland was like putting a saddle on a cow; the Poles thought it was like putting a yoke on a stallion. But to understand why socialism on the Soviet model has failed so overwhelmingly to establish itself securely in Poland, to appreciate why the working class, which should in theory be a socialist state's most loyal supporter, in fact has become a vanguard of opposition, it is necessary to look closely at what the government installed by Stalin was and was not able to accomplish after 1945.

There are two basic features that distinguish Poland from all its neighbors in Eastern Europe: the strength of its national Catholic Church and the predominance of private rather than collectivized agriculture. In the aftermath of the crushing of Solidarity as a legal nationwide organization, the Church is undoubtedly once again the single most important bulwark of opposition to socialism. Church services are often the occasion for demonstrations of national feeling and what the government would describe as political dissent. Many priests—particularly younger ones—make their church buildings available for a wide range of independent activities, such as debates, study groups, art exhibitions, or theater performances that cannot take place officially. From their pulpits, these outspoken young priests preach sermons in which they take the regime to task for its disregard for Christian values, national culture and what—following the teaching of the Polish Pope John Paul II—they describe as God-given human and civil rights.

One such priest was Father Jerzy Popiełuszko, chaplain to the Warsaw steel-workers, whose weekly "Masses for the Homeland" were attended by thousands of worshippers. His brutal murder at the hands of secret police in October 1984 appalled Polish (and world) public opinion and provoked a crisis in the regime itself. His killers were finally tried and sentenced to long terms of imprisonment.

The identification of the nation with the Catholic Church was forged in the crucible of foreign occupation during the partitions, when the Poles prayed fervently to "Mary, Queen of Poland," and hardened to the temper of gunmetal during the Nazi occupation, when more than 3,000 clergy died in concentration camps or prisons. It continued into the Stalinist period, when the country's great postwar primate, Stefan Cardinal Wyszyński, gave a personal demonstration of extraordinary fortitude. For a period of three years,

between 1953 and 1956, the authorities kept him under house arrest in a remote monastery. "I had feared that I would never share this honor, which has befallen all my colleagues," he noted in his diary on the first day of his captivity. "They have all experienced concentration camps and prisons."

But it was not only by defiance that the Catholic Church preserved and strengthened its position in the Communist state. Before he was arrested, Wyszyński had negotiated with the Stalinist government a far-reaching agreement in which he made a number of very substantial compromises—notably, by granting the authorities an effective veto on senior Church appointments. This pact was fiercely criticized by many Polish Catholics at the time.

Yet it was precisely the mixture of a readiness to compromise with an unyielding stubbornness on essentials that

Shoppers in Bodzentyn, near Kielce in southern Poland, crowd together in a bread line. Although chronic food shortages and erratic supplies are relieved to a small extent by the black market, those who can afford its prices are few; for the majority, waiting in line is the only alternative.

In the vaulted arcade of Kraków's
325-foot-long Cloth Hall, customers at
a café wait to give their orders. Originally a 14th-century covered market,
the Cloth Hall was rebuilt by Polish
and Italian masters during the Renaissance and today houses souvenir
shops and an art gallery.

brought the Church relatively unscathed through the darkest days.
Wyszyński had carefully observed the
ways in which the Church had been
crippled elsewhere in Eastern Europe
and concluded that his first priority
must be to preserve its institutional
structures: its buildings, seminaries
and religious orders. If the foundations
could be preserved, he thought, then
the religious superstructure could be
rebuilt in better times.

Subsequent events seem to have vin-
dicated his calculation. The authorities
backed away from enforcing anti-
Church policies by sheer physical terror, which Stalin had used in the 1930s
in the Soviet Union. Perhaps they
feared that in following Stalin's prac-
tices they would cut away the relatively
narrow branch of public support on
which they sat.

It is one of history's finer ironies that
Poland's Communist government actually contributed directly to the emer-
gence of a Polish pope. In 1964, under
the provisions of Wyszyński's Church-
state pact, the authorities vetoed several of the Church's proposed candidates
for the archbishopric of Kraków. The
nominee they finally accepted was Karol Wojtyła, later Pope John Paul II, a
man whose commitment to human and
civil rights was to play a major part in
the intellectual prehistory of Solidarity.
Also crucial to the birth of that movement was the pope's first extraordinary
pilgrimage to his native land in June
1979. Millions turned out to follow
him, listen to him and pray with him at
the great shrines of Polish Catholicism.
For nine incredible days, the state virtually ceased to exist, except as a censor
doctoring the television coverage.

So old and intimate is the mixture of
patriotism and religion in Poland that it

137

5

is almost impossible to separate them. The vast congregations singing the traditional hymns and reciting the old prayers demonstrate the strength of the Poles' faith; no one needs a hymn book or prayer book, everyone knows the words by heart. Such depth of faith is hard to find in most Western lands.

Poland is not the only country in which the phenomenon of Communism strengthens Christianity, but here the paradox is most acute. Lech Wałęsa once remarked: "If you look at what we Poles have in our pockets and in our shops, then Communism has done very little for us. But if you look at what is in our souls, I suggest that Communism has done a great deal for us. In fact, our souls contain exactly the opposite of what they wanted. They wanted us not to believe in God, and our churches are full. They wanted us to be materialistic and incapable of sacrifice: we are anti-materialistic and capable of sacrifice. They wanted us to be afraid of the tanks, of the guns, and instead we don't fear them at all."

Wałęsa gives an idealized picture. In fact, many younger Poles—and particularly those who have had higher education—display a strikingly selective attitude to the teachings of their pope and the Church: Their ears are acutely tuned to any note of political defiance but curiously deaf to the pope's strict teaching on sexual morality, for example; they hear what they want to hear and disregard the rest. On the other hand, particularly in the few years since martial law was imposed in December 1981, there have been signs of a purely religious revival. Thousands of young people have joined evangelistic and charismatic movements, attended Christian "retreats," and made group pilgrimages—often on foot—to such

holy places as the shrine of the Black Madonna in the fortress-like monastery of Jasna Góra at Częstochowa.

A skeptic could find cogent secular explanations for this phenomenon: an escape from the gray narrowness of material life, perhaps, or a search for an outlet for frustrated political aspirations. But whatever the cause, there is in Poland a dimension of faith that will not be found among the younger generation in the more prosperous and free societies of the West.

Nowhere are the traditional communities of faith more powerful than in the rural villages inhabited by that other bastion of Poland's uniqueness, the private peasantry. To travel into the Polish countryside is to step through a time warp into an earlier century. Traveling along the main road from Kraków to the economically backward southeastern region around Rzeszów, drivers constantly have to swerve perilously into the middle of the road to avoid horse-drawn carts loaded with timber, or elderly peasant women driving gaggles of geese. In the neighboring fields, the plows are also horse drawn. In the villages, the roads are dirt tracks.

Most of the houses in the villages are built of wood: They consist of two or three low-ceilinged, dark rooms, furnished with old metal bedframes and cheap reproductions of religious paintings on the walls. There usually are several color photographs of the pope as well. In winter, the whole family gathers to weave baskets by hand to supplement their meager income. In many cases, the only modern brick-and-mortar building in the whole village will be the church, filled every Sunday with row upon row of peasants, young and old, with creaking leather

boots and faces right out of Breughel.

Looking across the fields, the visitor sees an intricate patchwork quilt of tiny, fragmented plots. At first glance, the terrain looks like the result of centuries of land division stretching back to the Middle Ages. But in fact, this medieval landscape was created by the state immediately after World War II, when the government redistributed 14.8 million acres of land in tiny parcels, in a vain attempt to win the allegiance of the peasantry, which at the time was still a majority of the population. Subsequently, during the Stalinist period, the Polish government attempted to collectivize agriculture at Moscow's behest. Private farmers were persuaded or coerced to join wholly state-run collective farms. But in practice, only one tenth of the land was collectivized by 1956, and in the "Polish October" of that year, when the nation rallied behind a new leader, Władysław Gomułka, some four fifths of the collective farms that had been set up were spontaneously dissolved by their members. Today, 77 percent of Poland's agricultural land is still in private hands; the rest is divided between state and cooperative farms. Thus Poland's private farmers, like the Catholic Church, have preserved a unique position in the Warsaw Pact.

At the same time, the government has not given farmers the conditions they need to prosper. They have no lobby inside the power structure, and they have been consistently neglected and discriminated against—whether in the provision of building materials or fertilizers, the granting of modernization loans from the state banks (there are no others), or the right to social security or welfare provisions (until very recently the independent farmers had no state pensions). The production

Beneath his co-workers' clothing, hoisted out of the way on chains, a miner dresses in the changing room of a Silesian pit. Poland is the world's fourth-largest producer of coal; and its miners are among the country's most highly paid workers, earning three times the national average wage.

of agricultural machinery geared to the needs of private farmers was neglected; large tractors went primarily to state and cooperative farms—hence the use of horse-drawn plows. Tracts of land are uneconomically small; the average farm in Poland is still a tiny 12 acres. Yet despite all these obstacles, private farms are still, on the average, 25 percent more efficient than their state-owned or cooperative counterparts.

Following the industrial workers' example in 1980, many of Poland's 3.5 million private farmers did in fact get together to form their own union—Rural Solidarity. At Rzeszów in February 1981, the government signed an agreement with the farmers' representatives, in which the state undertook to end discrimination against the agricultural private sector and to improve supplies "until free market trade is fully restored." Since General Wojciech Jaruzelski's 1981 declaration of a "state of war" against the independent labor unions, Rural Solidarity activists, like their worker colleagues, have been harassed and imprisoned but the government has done much more to keep the promises of the Rzeszów agreement than it ever did to keep the terms of the agreement for the industrial workers that ended the 1980 Gdańsk strike. The government naturally wants to maintain the food supplies to the towns. Indeed, with improved state-procurement prices for their products, many private farmers have done very well materially in recent years. Although, as they are quick to point out, there is still not much available for them to buy with the bulging sacks of złotys hidden under their mattresses.

The reforms came too late to avert major shortages in the food supply, however. If private agriculture had

139

been given a free hand to modernize itself and farmers had been given the right to sell their produce on the free market, Poland might have been able to feed itself—and at a price people could have afforded. But shortages are frequent. They are exacerbated by a highly inefficient state-run distribution system—according to one estimate, one third of the country's milk production goes to waste, spoiled before it can be delivered—and by a system of unrealistic, state-fixed prices. The thriving black market can only partly compensate for the failings of the official system. Moreover, the subsidies that the government has had to provide to keep basic food prices low have put a tre-

mendous burden on the state budget. And when the authorities have needed to raise these prices, often quite sharply, the shock has inevitably triggered working-class protests that have shaken the state.

In the 1950s, Poland was a major food exporter. By the mid-1970s, it had become a large-scale importer of both food and fodder, partly to sustain a level of meat consumption that was well beyond its means. The regime believed such imports were necessary in order to buy popular acceptance. Food and fodder imports were a major contributor to the country's huge foreign debt (estimated at about $33 billion at the end of 1986). The failure to modernize ag-

riculture meant that Poland's industrial development was inevitably going to suffer its own setbacks.

The survival of an independent peasantry has been of great importance for the political sociology of the country. Against all Marxist dogma, these small landowners have developed close ties with their supposed enemy, the industrial working class. There are now more than four million people classified as peasant workers—that is, people who work in a factory for the day or during the week but live on a small farm at other times. When the harvest has to be brought in, these peasant workers simply fail to turn up at the workbench.

Moreover, every third urban worker

140

is the child of peasants—the first generation earning a living away from the land. Lech Wałęsa's father, for example, had a small farm that covered 7.5 acres in the Land of Dobrzyń near Włocławek in northeastern Poland. And Wałęsa, like millions more, took with him into the industrial city many of the traditional values and the long-held patriotic religiosity of the independent peasantry.

The Polish state—in common with the other states of the Soviet bloc—claims to have achieved the industrialization of its country. Its evidence is presented in statistics of increased coal and steel production, miles of railroad tracks laid and apartment complexes built. According to official statistics, 68 percent of the population lived on the land in 1946 and only 42 percent were living there in 1978. Farmers now account for less than one third of the work force.

There is no denying the truth of the claim, and for the first generation of peasants who flocked from the overpopulated, impoverished countryside to find work in the new industries, the change meant a significant improvement in their standard of living. From cramped wooden houses along dirt tracks, they moved into new apartment buildings—not palaces, but built of concrete and equipped with indoor plumbing. For the first time, such workers had basic health care and social security. And this big step up in the world gave many a sense of indebtedness to the industrial system.

Yet from early on, the way in which Poland adopted industrialization was deeply flawed, carrying with it the seeds of the economic disorders that are so visible today. During the Stalinist period, from 1949 to 1954, the system

of centralized planning was established. Excessive emphasis was placed on primary and heavy industry, and much of this development—the extraction of Silesian coal and other raw materials and the production of iron and steel—was geared to the immediate needs of the armaments industry and the Soviet Union. Moreover, the planners had a strong preference for vast new factories, often placed in underdeveloped regions of the country.

A classic example is the "model town" of Nowa Huta, laid out in the 1950s around the New Lenin Steelworks near Kraków, a very long way from the Silesian coalfields on which it depends. The development was sited there to provide jobs for the peasant workers of the southeast and to serve as a proletarian counterweight to the old Catholic and royalist city of Kraków, that hotbed of middle-class Catholic values. In this political purpose it backfired, however, for the first cause that really united the workers of Nowa Huta was their demand for a church. The authorities fought long and hard to prevent it, but they finally had to give in. To this day, the workers will describe with pleasure how they "borrowed" the bulldozers and tractors from the factory in order to dig the foundations for the Church of Mary, Queen of Poland. Present-day Nowa Huta has three large modern churches, and they are filled every Sunday.

The idea of concentrating the workers in enormous industrial complexes was partly intended to form massed regiments of proletarian support for the new regime. When that support failed to materialize, the new towns quickly became bastions of opposition. But they were not the first flash points when trouble came. The initial out-

burst of protest occurred in Poznań (until 1918 the German-Polish city of Posen), which had a comparatively old and established industry and also some tradition of labor militancy. Here, in June 1956, workers went into the streets to protest their rapidly deteriorating economic position. Internal security forces put down the uprising in two days of fighting, during which at least 53 people were killed.

Later that year, a large group of Polish economists advanced pioneering proposals for reforming an economy suffering from the overcentralized command. Many of their recommendations were adopted by the government; for a time, it seemed that the situation might improve. But the economists' programs were frustrated by a combination of bureaucratic inertia and vested interests. Władysław Gomułka demonstrated limited imagination in sponsoring the reforms; perhaps, too, he wanted to show that, at least in the industrial sector, Poland could stick to Soviet models. The continued concentration on heavy primary industry meant that the workers rarely saw the fruits of their labor in the form of consumer goods. Nor did their spending power grow appreciably. According to Polish economist Włodzimierz Brus, the annual increase in real wages in the course of the 1960s, a boom period for Europe, was "not even statistically significant."

In December 1970, just two weeks before Christmas, the government suddenly announced that staple food prices would be increased by as much as 36 percent. The response was an earthquake of working-class protest that toppled Gomułka and shook the whole regime to its foundations. There were

5

strikes across much of the country. Several big Warsaw factories were occupied by their workers. But the bloodshed came in the Baltic ports of Gdańsk, Gdynia and Szczecin, where armed police and professional soldiers shot and killed workers.

At the Lenin Shipyard in Gdańsk, a giant socialist enterprise with more than 15,000 employees, the shock of the shooting in front of the shipyard gates united the work force of raw peasant sons into a cohesive community for the first time. To the shipyard workers, with their mixture of patriotic peasant piety and proletarian self-respect bred by socialism, their martyred colleagues—Poles murdered by Poles, workers murdered by a "workers' state"—became the symbol for all their accummulated grievances.

Nonetheless, after the new party leader, Edward Gierek, had come in person to the shipyards and apologized for the party's mistakes, the workers once again promised the party their support. "I am only a worker like you," Gierek said. "Will you help us?" he asked. "We will help you!" shouted back the workers.

Gierek used their support to attempt to push Poland through a second industrial revolution—he himself talked of building a "second Poland." Growth was fueled with technology and machinery imported from the West and paid for by Western loans. The theory was that goods from the new factories would then be exported back to the West to earn the hard currency to pay back the loans. Gierek intended that the payoff for Poland would be a steadily rising standard of living, which would be reflected in the shops in the form of consumer goods and be added to the traditional socialist advantages of full employment, social security and the stability of prices.

Gierek's broad economic strategy was neither unique nor intrinsically wrong; both János Kádár in Hungary and Erich Honecker in East Germany developed models of a "consumer socialism" at the same time. What was unique about Gierek's planned "great leap forward" was its scale, the breathtaking incompetence with which it was executed, the lack of a properly modernized agricultural base to support it, and, last but by no means least, the recalcitrant society he had to deal with. For a short time, his formula seemed to be working: Poland experienced a consumer boom. By the mid-1970s, however, it was already clear that things were going badly. In June 1976, the government had to raise staple food prices again. Strikes and street protests were the immediate result. This time the party leader survived in office, but only by withdrawing the price increases almost immediately.

From then until the summer of 1980, Gierek and his colleagues were like the pilots of an airliner that has gone into a nose dive. They tried every trick they knew, but the machine would not respond to the controls. The dive became steeper and steeper; the pointer on the hard-currency dial whirled into the red, from the $10-billion mark in 1976 to about $17 billion in 1979. Meanwhile, shortages increased and people felt they were getting poorer.

This economic failure, with the traditional trigger of food price hikes, led directly to the fourth great explosion of working-class anger in the summer of 1980. This time the workers did not cry "We will help you!" They had given the state its chance in 1956 and 1970; now they would help themselves.

A striking worker gazes thoughtfully through the gates of the Lenin Shipyard in Gdańsk during a Sunday-morning open-air mass in August 1980. That month, the government signed a 21-point agreement with the workers, conceding their demands for new self-governing unions.

Yet by the early 1980s, it was a different "they" from the untrained, new working class of the early 1950s. For a start, the young workers who were the driving force in Solidarity were better educated than the first generation of peasants straight off the land. Free compulsory education for everyone was, after all, one of the basic modernizing and equalizing reforms introduced by the postwar state. What is more, through this education, and through the ubiquitous propaganda, the new generation had been indoctri-

FILMING THE BIRTH PANGS OF SOLIDARITY

During the filming of *Man of Iron*, director Andrzej Wajda, in the red sweater, sets up a shot with his camera crew. They are re-creating a scene that took place in front of the Lenin Shipyard at the start of the strike.

During the brief time that Poland's free labor union, Solidarity, was sanctioned—from August 1980 until December 1981—artists of all kinds benefited from a thaw in the climate of political censorship. The results were particularly noticeable in the filmmaking industry, which became one of the most effective channels for disseminating the spirit of the Solidarity movement.

Foremost among the directors to exploit the new mood was the world-renowned Andrzej Wajda. One of his early films, *Man of Marble*, dealt with a bricklayer, who was decorated in Stalinist days as a hero of labor, then fell from political grace. In the sequel, *Man of Iron*, the bricklayer's son becomes a Solidarity leader. Despite the film's controversial content, it was approved by the Ministry of Culture and was shot in just six weeks. The movie was a prizewinner at the Cannes Film Festival, and more significantly, it was hailed by the Poles themselves, playing to packed houses even at 5 a.m. screenings.

nated in and had internalized certain recognizably socialist tenets.

The newspapers, television, schoolteachers and party leaders had told them again and again that they, the workers, were the rulers now. They had been taught that in a socialist state all property belongs to the people. They had been led to believe that a socialist state should institutionalize equality: equality in education, health care, job opportunity and income. But it was clear the present rulers were not practicing what they preached. The

party, not the workers, ruled; property belonged to the state not to society; and the greatest offense, inequality in income, education, health care and job opportunity, grew in the 1970s.

It was characteristic of the Gierek era that the society's gains were unevenly distributed. Relatively speaking, the rich got richer and the poor got poorer. According to a report by a group of independent experts, the income differential in Poland in the 1970s was 20 to 1. Moreover, those who benefited from this inequality were primarily the

members of the party power elite.

Following the example of other countries of the Soviet bloc, Poland extended the application of the Russian term for the lists of jobs under control of the party—the *nomenklatura*—to the people filling the posts: central and local government officials, managers in industry, publishers, newspaper editors, army officers, labor leaders, teachers and academics, bankers, leaders of youth and of women's organizations, judges, even fire chiefs. All in all, there are probably some 200,000 to 300,000

5

nomenklatura jobs in Poland. With families and dependents, this classification applies to perhaps 1.5 million people.

The *nomenklatura* is one very important way in which the Soviet Union secures its domination over Eastern Europe. Its members have a vested stake in the stability of the system, which is the source and guarantee of their personal welfare. It promises them a position of relative affluence and security that many of them could not hope to achieve on merit in a free society.

The *nomenklatura* can accurately be described as a client ruling class. Its members enjoy power, status and privileges simply by belonging to it. In Poland, this ruling elite has a characteristic appearance. The faces that stare out of the solemn black-and-white portrait photographs in the main party daily newspaper, *Trybuna Ludu (Tribune of the People),* overwhelmingly display the broad, Slav features and pendulous jowls of peasant sons who have not lifted a spade for 30 years, except at a ceremonial opening of some prestigious building project or perhaps to dig the gardens of their comfortable private villas. These people sit securely in their offices, occupying all the commanding heights of the economy, politics and social life.

Under Gierek, who had once worked as a miner in Belgium and France, the *nomenklatura* were allowed to improve their own situations with the help of a licensed corruption that is characteristic of life in most Soviet-bloc countries. Senior officials and functionaries used state labor, materials and equipment—all originally intended for the construction of public housing—to build themselves luxurious villas, hunting lodges and saunas. Working-class people referred bitterly to these self-satisfied ap-

Seen from the tower of the Church of Our Lady, the rebuilt houses of Gdańsk's 14th-century Main Town extend to the Motlawa River. More than 90 percent of old Gdańsk was destroyed in World War II.

paratchiks as "the owners of the People's Poland."

As a result, the brightest and most energetic among the new generation of peasant workers were unable to advance from the shop floor to positions of higher status, income and responsibility—even though they were much better educated than most of the people who occupied those positions. This artificially blocked social mobility, and the reservoir of frustrated talent that it created on the shop floors of giant enterprises like Nowa Huta or the Huta Warszawa Steelworks, goes a long way to explain the energy and articulateness of the young workers' leaders in Solidarity.

They attacked the inequality, corruption and inefficiency of the ruling class with an acid anger. The formula for that acid was one part direct, everyday material frustration; one part socialist education; and one part traditional values of patriotic Catholicism. The final element in this explosive cocktail was quantitatively very small but qualitatively very important: the influence of what may be called the "intellectual opposition."

The intelligentsia in Poland is two rather different things; it is both an official sociological category and a tradition. The officially recognized class includes all those with higher education. The tradition is somewhat more selective. It defines the true intellectuals or members of the intelligentsia by how they behave rather than merely by formal schooling. Tradition never forgets the aristocratic origins of the Polish intellectual heritage among younger sons and poorer members of the landed classes in the late 18th and early 19th centuries. Its ethos can be, in part, a kind of snobbery; members are recog-

ALKOHOL = ABSENCJA

Empty overalls highlight the problem of alcohol-related job absenteeism.

CYRK

A clown's head and bowler merge in this circus poster.

WITOLD GOMBROWICZ

TEATR NOWY W ŁODZI

OPERETKA

The torso of a woman doubles as an operagoer's face.

THE EXUBERANCE OF POSTER ART

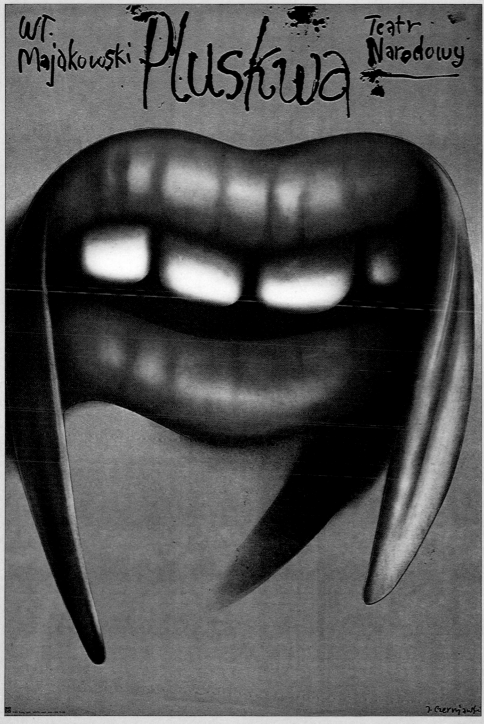

A play called *The Bedbug* is advertised with a menacing image of sinister fanged lips.

For graphic power and originality of conception, Polish poster design has few equals. It has long been recognized as both a sophisticated art form and a powerfully effective means of getting messages across to the public.

The history of the poster in Poland dates back to the 1890s, but its golden age began after World War II and reached its apogee in the 1970s, when the works shown here were produced. Although influenced by such international trends as surrealism and pop art, the images draw their power from the designer's individual vision. They also share what is a typically Polish characteristic: a subtle and eccentric humor.

Enlightened state and public patronage has encouraged freedom to experiment and permitted the results to be seen on billboards throughout the country, where they advertise plays, political rallies, poetry readings and jazz concerts among other events. Originality and inventiveness are further encouraged by competitions and prizes. In Warsaw, four annual prizes are awarded for the best posters to be seen on the capital's streets; and once every two years, the city acts as host to the cream of Polish and world poster talent at the International Poster Biennale.

Not surprisingly, the most famous recent example of Polish graphic design has had little support from the state. The logotype of the Solidarity movement—bold red letters proclaiming the Polish word *solidarność*—was conceived by a young Gdańsk designer, Jerzy Janiszewski. It has been banned since the imposition of martial law and can be legally displayed only in churches.

Passengers traveling along the Elbląg Canal in northern Poland watch from the deck as their vessel is towed over a hill on tracks connecting one stretch of water with the next. Five such portages take the place of locks on the 90-mile-long canal.

nized by the quality of their spoken Polish, by their glass-fronted bookcases, by their manners and even by the way they smoke their cigarettes (held vertically between forefinger and thumb). But more important, they also carry a sense of a very special moral and patriotic responsibility. Throughout the 123 years of the partitions, it was the intelligentsia that kept alive the idea and ideals of Polishness in culture, especially in literature and education, against the best efforts of the German, Austro-Hungarian and Russian empires to suppress them. Contemporary Polish writers remember that the great 19th-century Romantic poets were known as Poland's "spiritual government."

That is Poland's great tradition, one of high-minded opposition to the alien, secular powers that be: the pen against the sword. The intelligentsia, however, has not always been as broadly and as strongly opposed to the regime as it is today. In the first decade after World War II, many of Poland's intellectuals more or less enthusiastically supported the new Communist regime. Some hoped that they could, after all, build some specifically Polish variety of socialism; others delighted in attacking the "obscurantist" and "reactionary" Catholic Church. Sobered by the experience of Stalinism, many nevertheless set out during and after the Polish October of 1956 to reform the system through the party.

> *For a clear truth,*
> *For the bread of freedom,*
> *For ardent reason.*
> *We demand this every day.*
> *We demand through the party.*

So wrote Adam Ważyk in a poem that best summarizes the intellectual spirit

A CHRONOLOGY OF KEY EVENTS

800-900 A.D. West Slavic tribes of the Oder and Vistula river basins unite under the Polanie, a tribe that gives rise to Poland's first ruling dynasty, the Piast. The tribes become known collectively as Poles.

962-992 Under the first recorded Piast prince, Mieszko I, Christianity is promulgated among the Poles.

992-1025 Mieszko's son, Bolesław I (the Brave), vastly extends his realm and is crowned first king of Poland in 1025. After his death, Poland becomes fragmented into warring factions.

1333-1370 Medieval Poland emerges as a prosperous European power under the last Piast king, Casimir the Great. The law is codified, trade is fostered and the University of Kraków is founded in 1364.

1410 Combined Polish-Lithuanian armies defeat the Knights of the Teutonic Order at the Battle of Grünwald; another defeat in 1454 gives Poland access to the Baltic Sea and establishes the port of Gdańsk as a "free city" under Polish suzerainty.

1543 The Polish astronomer Nicolaus Copernicus' work *On the Revolutions of the Celestial Spheres* shocks the scientific establishment with its theory that the earth circles the sun.

1572 The death without heir of Sigismund II (the August) ends the Jagiellonian line; successive elected monarchs involve Poland in disastrous wars with Swedes, Russians and Cossacks.

1772 In the first partition of Poland, Russia, Prussia and Austria take advantage of Polish anarchy, political strife and lack of a standing army, to annex one third of its territory.

1793 Russia and Prussia force a second partition of Poland, causing a national insurrection—led by the Polish officer Tadeusz Kościuszko—in 1794.

1795 In a third partition, the final third of Poland is divided among Russia, Prussia and Austria, erasing Poland from the map of Europe.

1807 Napoleon I creates the Duchy of Warsaw from land held by Prussia.

1815 The Congress of Vienna ratifies the division of Poland; the Duchy of Warsaw is renamed the Kingdom of Poland—often called Congress Poland—and is united with Russia.

1830-1831 An uprising in Russian-held Poland against the autocratic Tsar Nicholas I of Russia is crushed; some 10,000 Poles are forced into exile. When he hears that Russian forces have taken Warsaw, the Polish composer Frédéric Chopin writes his *Revolutionary Étude* for piano.

1864 Tsar Alexander II frees the peasants of Congress Poland.

1918 On November 11, the Polish Republic is proclaimed; the Polish pianist Ignacy Jan Paderewski becomes premier.

1926 Marshal Piłsudski becomes virtual dictator of Poland after a military coup.

1939 After Hitler concludes a secret pact with Stalin to split Poland between them, German troops invade Poland on September 1, precipitating World War II; on September 17, Soviet forces attack Poland from the east.

1940 Thousands of Polish officers are massacred by the Russians in the forest of Katyn, near Smolensk.

1943 An armed uprising by the Jews of the Warsaw Ghetto is crushed after a desperate four-week fight.

1944 The Polish Home Army leads a Warsaw uprising that lasts two months before surrendering to the Germans.

1945 Soviet troops liberate Poland and enter the razed city of Warsaw.

1947 Poland holds its first general elections. The Soviet-sponsored Polish Workers' party is the strongest party.

1949 Poland joins Comecon.

1956 A workers' rebellion in Poznań leaves 54 dead. Władysław Gomułka is appointed party leader.

1970 The Warsaw-Bonn Treaty defines Poland's border along the Oder-Neisse. A bloody workers' revolt in the Baltic ports topples Gomułka; leadership goes to Edward Gierek.

1978 The archbishop of Kraków, Karol Wojtyla, is elected Pope John Paul II.

1980 The independent labor union Solidarity is founded in Gdańsk, led by Lech Wałęsa. Nationwide strikes force Gierek to give in to the workers' demands, expressed in the Gdańsk Agreement.

1981-1982 Authorities establish market-oriented reforms. Implementation is hampered as General Jaruzelski, the prime minister, declares martial law; Solidarity is suspended in December and its leaders are held. Ten months later, Solidarity is dissolved by law.

1983 Martial law is lifted, but political curbs remain. Lech Wałęsa is awarded the Nobel Peace Prize.

1986 Poland joins International Monetary Fund and World Bank. Jaruzelski announces the second stage of market-oriented economic reforms and begins an amnesty program for political prisoners.

1987 The United States lifts all economic sanctions imposed to protest the dissolution of Solidarity between 1981 and 1982.

of that time. It was to take a decade of slow stagnation and disillusionment before most of them abandoned the hope that change and reform would come from within the establishment.

In March 1968, as a result of complex interfactional struggles inside the party, a vicious official campaign was launched against independent-minded students and professors, some of them Jewish, and against Jewish members of the party apparat. This campaign was officially described as "anti-Zionist"; to most observers it was obviously anti-Semitic. For many people, the campaign appeared to confirm the reputation for anti-Semitism that Poland had acquired before the war. In this case, however, the campaign was not of popular origin nor was it popular in practice. Some of Poland's most distinguished scholars were fired from Polish universities, and some of their brightest students were expelled. Thousands of Jews were barred from any further employment and were forced to emigrate.

In the same year, on the other side of the High Tatra, Soviet tanks rolled into Prague, crushing the Czechoslovaks' hopes of reform through the party. After these two devastating episodes, most of Poland's leading intellectuals finally abandoned their earlier thoughts of any significant liberalization and democratization coming from inside the political establishment. Instead, they began to look for ways of changing the system by exerting pressure from the outside.

Throughout the 1970s, in the relatively tolerant conditions that the Gierek regime allowed, a number of small opposition groups were formed. Historically, the most important was the Workers' Defense Committee, known by its Polish initials as KOR. It was es-

Visiting Poland in June of 1983, Pope John Paul II rides through a huge crowd gathered for Mass in Warsaw's sports arena. This was the pontiff's second trip to his homeland after his election in 1978 as the first non-Italian pope in 450 years.

tablished in the autumn of 1976 to help workers who were being victimized for the part they had taken in protesting food price increases earlier that year. It was KOR that argued most clearly that the only way for Poles to win lasting changes was to organize themselves outside the aegis of the party-state. KOR's members dreamed that such a movement of "social self-defense" could gradually expand the areas of pluralism and self-determination inside Poland, while continued party control of foreign, defense and security policy would reassure Moscow. KOR was also instrumental in helping to bring about the vital reconciliation between the once militantly atheistic Left and the Church. Faced with the common enemy of a totalitarian state, KOR member Adam Michnik argued, it was now absolutely imperative that the two traditions unite in the defense of their shared values: respect for human rights and human dignity.

KOR was unique among the opposition groups in the attention it paid to developing links with the working class. In the late 1970s, it drew attention to the worsening conditions of the industrial work force and encouraged the creation of unofficial labor union committees to demand improvements. The free labor union committee formed by KOR on the Baltic coast was to be instrumental in initiating and leading the strike at Gdańsk's Lenin Shipyard in August of 1980.

The coming together of so many elements—rural tradition and urban experience, socialism and Catholicism, intellectuals and workers—has made Polish society what it is today. So has the country's extraordinary demography. With one of the highest birth rates in Europe in recent years, 50 percent of Poland's 37 million people are under 30 years of age. Poland is an old nation of young people, unsure of what the future holds.

Materially speaking, their condition is poor by comparison with Hungary or Czechoslovakia, let alone with Western Europe. By the late 1980s, food shortages and lines were not as dramatic as they were in 1981, but meat is still rationed, the range of available goods is narrow and—as a new development—even basic items are expensive. Most working couples will spend at least one of their salaries on groceries and household necessities. It is possible to supplement the meager official supplies with food bought on the black market, which is widely tolerated by the local authorities, but the laws of supply and demand often make such goods five or even 10 times as expensive as those in the state-operated shops. Clothes and hardware are in even shorter supply, and it is not unusual for people to wait years for such consumer durables as a washing machine or a refrigerator. As for housing, the average waiting period for an apartment is now more than 15 years. Young families often have to live in one or two small rooms in the corner of a parent's apartment.

The economic crisis has also, inevitably, wreaked its vengeance on the nation's health. Poles are less well nourished than they used to be. The average annual per capita consumption of meat fell from 155 pounds in 1975 to 127 pounds in 1983. Egg and milk consumption also fell, with the result that the average Pole's protein intake in the mid-1980s was lower than that in 1970. This protein deficiency places children particularly at risk. The national health service lacks the staff, the equipment

A member of Poland's motorized antiriot militia, deployed during the 1983 papal visit, checks his camera's light meter while his colleagues keep a sharp eye on bystanders lining the route. The 30,000-strong militia's tactics have made it a target for popular resentment.

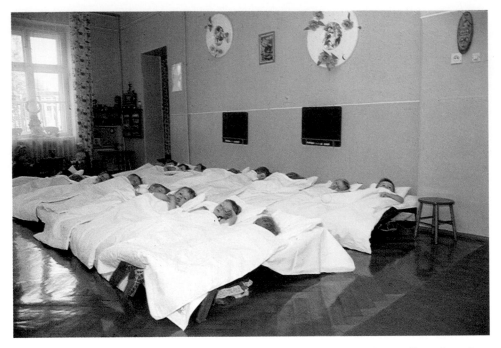

and the money to cope with the resulting increase in demand for its services; there are not enough hospitals, just as there are not enough schools. The state's dire hard-currency debt means that the health service is starved of the dollars needed for foreign drugs and equipment. Western charity—truckloads of medical supplies, food and clothing parcels—manages to make up only a small part of the difference.

The ordinary family may not understand the macroeconomic causes for the failings of the health and education services. But they know the consequences. They know what it means for a mother to have to give birth without anesthetic in a dirty hospital ward with only one overworked and exhausted midwife in attendance; they know what it means for that baby to risk growing up with anemia. They may also learn what it means for a child to have to go to school at 4 o'clock in the afternoon because enrollment is so overcrowded that the school day is divided into three shifts.

The state never tires of repeating that there is no unemployment in Po-

land. But there is the reality of underemployment, which is almost as demoralizing. Shop assistants stand idle all day because there are no goods to sell. In factories, production lines may be at a standstill for hours on end, for want of some vital part or raw material. With nothing better to do, the workers play cards and drink tea—or vodka. Alcoholism is a national health problem.

Moreover, people have no feeling that they are working for themselves. The government has tried to give them a sense of participation through new, official labor unions set up to replace Solidarity, but most people regard these as frauds and as no substitute for the banned independent union.

The combined effect is one of profound distress, alienation and demoralization. Yet, somehow, everyday life goes on. Despite the shortages, Polish women still manage to dress with a sense of style that far surpasses their counterparts in many a Western country. And most Saturday evenings still find young Poles gathered in crowded apartments for those spontaneous and unstructured parties—*imprezy,* in stu-

dent slang—that are the most typical form of urban social life. There will be vodka or wine to drink and a few open-faced sandwiches to eat; later, the parquet floor will vibrate to the beat of the dancing. Then on Sunday morning, the same people will probably go to church and confess the "sins" of the night before.

In the summer, a typical working-class family may enjoy two or three weeks in the summer on the wide sandy beaches along the Baltic. Members of the intelligentsia quite often spend as long as two months away, often staying in small cottages in the wooded foothills of the Tatra Mountains in the south, where Pope John Paul was born. And in the winter in those mountains, there is excellent skiing, which the pope himself used to enjoy.

Polish life is certainly not all grayness and crisis. Indeed, the less satisfaction the Poles derive from their public and working lives, the more time and effort they are able to invest in private and social pleasures. Foreign visitors are often surprised to find an ease, a warmth and even a leisurely pace that contrasts with the bustle of Western consumer societies.

It is often said that Poland is a deeply divided society. Most Poles would not agree. They would say that Poland is a deeply united society—united against its government. Indeed the very word "society" is most often used in Polish in this sense: "the society" (*społeczénstwo*) as opposed to "the power" (*władza*). This is, of course, a simplification: Besides the *nomenklatura,* there are people—particularly elderly people—who more or less actively support the government and are driven by a variety of motives, ranging from fear and avarice to a genuine patriotism.

FOLK TRADITIONS LOVINGLY PRESERVED

In the mountainous region of Podhale, in the shadow of the slopes of the Tatra range, live 150,000 highlanders—the *górale*. Sheltered by their geography, they have preserved a unique folk culture of traditional crafts and brilliantly colorful decorative arts. Nowhere are old customs more zealously maintained than in *górale* weddings, at which guests wear their finest embroidered costumes and the music and feasting may continue for a whole week.

Yet for centuries, life was hard for this close-knit community, eking a scanty living from inhospitable soil; by 1910, hunger had forced one fifth of the population to emigrate to the United States. Today, prospects are brighter. As well as farming, the highlanders work in factories or practice their native crafts under government sponsorship.

A *górale* bride and groom wear richly embroidered folk costumes for their wedding.

5

Despite the crushing of the Solidarity movement, there is still a great deal of solidarity, with a small *s*, to be found. In spite of the repression and impoverishment in the years since the imposition of martial law, there remains a spirit of defiance. More than any other nation in Eastern Europe, the Poles are a people united by a sense of what they want, even if, since the supression of Solidarity, they have no more idea than anyone else of how they are to achieve it.

The party, furthermore, has not yet reestablished its control over all the areas of life that it controlled prior to 1980—or at the height of the Stalinist period nearly 30 years before. The forums where people are permitted to say what they think are still considerably larger in Poland than in Czechoslovakia and even, it can be argued, larger than in Hungary: for example, in many universities and in the great range of cultural activities sponsored or protected by the Church. The strength of the Roman Catholic Church, and the authorities' still-acute fear of widespread dissent, may ensure that some of these freedoms are preserved.

If the government cannot improve the people's material situation, and if it continues to deny them any serious participation in political and economic life, then there is a great danger that popular frustration will sooner or later spill over into another explosion of protest. This time, it could well be violent. But there is still a chance that the familiar Polish cycle of insurrection and repression may be averted, if only because people on all sides—the Church leaders, most of the opposition leaders, and probably most party and government leaders—are now so acutely aware of the danger and are determined to prevent it. □

A visitor to the Baltic Sea resort of Sopot suns herself on a pier while other tourists watch local boats. Poland's coast stretches 310 miles, from the mouth of the Oder River to the Gulf of Gdańsk, and attracts many vacationers to its sandy beaches and unspoiled fishing villages.

ACKNOWLEDGMENTS

The index was prepared by Vicki Robinson. For their assistance in the preparation of this volume, the editors also wish to thank: Nicholas G. Andrews, Chevy Chase, Maryland; Neal Ascherson, London; Mike Brown, London; Veronica Burger, London; Liza Caldwell, London; Čedok Limited, London; F. Cuba, Slušovice, Czechoslovakia; Czechoslovak Embassy, London; Vladislav Dřvota, Prague; Embassy of the Polish People's Republic, London; Neyla Freeman, London; John Gaisford, London; Helen Grubin, London; Henry Marchant Limited, London; Hungarian Embassy, London; Josef Hurta, Slušovice, Czechoslovakia; Mirec Jungr, Prague; B. W. Mazur, London; Capt. W. Milewski, Ursula McLean, London; Gwen C. Mullen, Alexandria, Virginia; Robin Olson, London; Roy Perrot, London; The Polish Institute and Sikorski Museum, London; Jayne E. Rohrich, Alexandria, Virginia; Kathleen Scanlan, International Trade Administration, Washington, D.C.; School of Slavonic and East European Studies, London; David Short, London; Jasmine Spencer, London; Father Szymon Stefanowicz, Częstochowa, Poland; Andrzej and Krystyna Strama, Poronin, Poland; Deborah Thompson, London; Agnieszka Wasak, Warsaw.

PICTURE CREDITS

Credits from left to right are separated by semicolons, from top to bottom by dashes.

Cover: Christopher Pillitz, London.
Front endpaper: Map by Roger Stewart, London. Back endpaper: Digitized map by Ralph Scott/Chapman Bounford, London.

1, 2: © Flag Research Center, Winchester, Massachusetts. 6, 7: Hans Wiesenhofer, Vienna, inset chart by John Drummond. 8, 9: Bruno Barbey from Magnum, Paris. 10, 11: Bill Weems from Woodfin Camp Inc., Washington, D.C. 12, 13: Bruno Barbey from Magnum, Paris, inset chart by John Drummond. 14, 15: Karol Kállay from Slovart, Bratislava, Czechoslovakia. 16, 17: Bill Weems from Woodfin Camp Inc., Washington, D.C. 18: Digitized map by Ralph Scott/Chapman Bounford, London. 19: Leonard Freed from Magnum, Paris. 20-25: Hans Wiesenhofer, Vienna. 26-31: Karol Kállay from Slovart, Bratislava, Czechoslovakia. 32: Bruno Barbey from Magnum, Paris. 33: Christopher Pillitz, London. 35: Bruno Barbey from Magnum, Paris. 36, 37: Tim Sharman, Battle, East Sussex, England. 38, 39: Bruno Barbey from Magnum, Paris. 40: Courtesy of the University Library, Prague, photo Mary Evans Picture Library, London. 43: Courtesy of the Uniwersytet Jagielłónski, Kraków, Poland, photo Bildarchiv Jürgens, Cologne, West Germany. 44, 45: José F. Poblete, Frankfurt, West Germany, inset courtesy of Magyar Nemzeti Múzeum, Budapest, photo Gyarmathy László, Budapest. 46: Engraving courtesy of the Národní galerie, Prague. 48, 49: Courtesy of Múzeum Naredowe, Warsaw, photo Centralna Agencia Fotograficzna, Warsaw; digitized maps by Chapman Bounford, London. 50: Watercolor courtesy of Národní galerie, Prague. 51: BBC Hulton Picture Library, London. 52: From *Pamatnik VII Sletu Vsesokolskeno Upraze, 1920,* pub. 1921, School of Slavonic and East European Studies, London. 53: BBC Hulton Picture Library, London. 55: Ullstein Bilderdienst, Berlin. 56-59: The Photo Source, London. 60, 61: Erich Lessing from Magnum, Paris (2)—BBC Hulton Picture Library, London. 62, 63: BBC Hulton Picture Library, London; Christopher Pillitz, London. 64, 65: Courtesy Fred Grunfeld, Majorca; Christopher Pillitz, London. 66, 67: Karol Kállay from Slovart, Bratislava, Czechoslovakia; Camera Press Ltd., London. 68-79: Hans Wiesenhofer, Vienna, except 77 right center: Bill Weems from Woodfin Camp Inc., Washington, D.C. 80: Bill Weems from Woodfin Camp Inc., Washington, D.C.; Camera Press Ltd., London. 81: Bill Weems from Woodfin Camp Inc., Washington, D.C. 82, 83: Leonard Freed from Magnum, Paris. 84: Bill Weems from Woodfin Camp Inc., Washington, D.C. 85-89: Hans Wiesenhofer, Vienna. 90, 91: Leonard Freed from Magnum, Paris. 92-101: Hans Wiesenhofer, Vienna. 102, 103: Peter Cook from Rapho, Paris. 105: Karol Kállay from Slovart, Bratislava, Czechoslovakia. 107: Christopher Pillitz, London. 108, 109: Karol Kállay from Slovart, Bratislava, Czechoslovakia (2); Christopher Pillitz, London. 110: Christopher Pillitz, London. 111: Marilyn Silverstone from Magnum, Paris. 112, 113: Karol Kállay, from Slovart, Bratislava, Czechoslovakia. 114: Christopher Pillitz, London. 115: José F. Poblete, Frankfurt, West Germany. 116: Mary Evans Picture Library, London; Christopher Pillitz, London. 118-121: Christopher Pillitz, London. 122: Sven Simon, Essen, West Germany. 123: Christopher Pillitz, London. 125: Karol Kállay from Slovart, Bratislava, Czechoslovakia. 126-135: Christopher Pillitz, London. 136: Bruno Barbey from Magnum, Paris. 137: Christopher Pillitz, London. 139: Bruno Barbey from Magnum, Paris. 140: Christopher Pillitz, London. 142: Peter Marlow from Magnum, Paris. 143-145: Bruno Barbey from Magnum, Paris. 146, 147: Photo Michał Sielewicz, Warsaw. 148: Bruno Barbey from Magnum, Paris. 150-152: Bildarchiv Jürgens, Cologne, West Germany. 153: Christopher Pillitz, London. 154, 155: Bruno Barbey from Magnum, Paris.

BIBLIOGRAPHY

BOOKS

Adelman, Jonathan R., *Terror and Communist Politics: The Role of the Secret Police in Communist States.* Boulder, Colorado: Westview Press, 1984.

Ascherson, Neal, *The Polish August.* London: Penguin, 1981.

Bajcar, Adam, *Poland.* Warsaw: Interpress, 1977.

Barbey, Bruno, *Portrait of Poland.* London: Thames and Hudson, 1982.

Baring-Gould, Sabine, *The Book of Were-Wolves.* London: Smith, Elder and Company, 1865.

Bojko, Szymon, *Polska Sztuka Plakatu.* Warsaw: Wydawnictwo Artystyczno Graficzne, 1971.

Clapham, John, *Antonín Dvořák.* London: Faber & Faber, 1966.

Davies, Norman, *Heart of Europe. A Short History of Poland.* Oxford, England: Clarendon Press, 1984.

Enyedi, Gyorgy, *Hungary.* Boulder, Colorado: Westview Press, 1977.

Gilbert, Martin, *The Holocaust.* London: Woburn House, 1978.

Griffiths, Paul, *Bartók.* London: J. M. Dent & Sons Ltd., 1984.

Halász, Zoltán, *The Book of Hungarian Wines.* Budapest: Corvina, 1980.

Hašek, Jaroslav, *The Good Soldier Švejk.* London: Penguin, 1978.

Hayman, Ronald, *Kafka: A Biography.* London: Abacus, 1983.

Heine, Marc, *Poland.* London: B. T. Batsford Ltd., 1980.

Hermann, A. H., *A History of the Czechs.* London: Allen Lane, 1975.

Hungary: Economic Developments and Reforms. Washington, D.C.: The World Bank, 1984.

Ignotus, Paul, *Hungary.* London: Ernest Benn, 1972.

Jackson, Michael, *The World Guide to Beer.* London: Mitchell Beazley, 1977.

Kádár, János, *Selected Speeches and Interviews.* Oxford, England: Pergamon Press, 1985.

Kafka, Franz, *Letters to Friends, Family and Editors.* London: John Calder, 1978.

Korbel, Josef, *Twentieth-Century Czechoslovakia.* New York: Columbia University Press, 1977.

Kundera, Milan, *The Joke.* London: Faber & Faber, 1983.

Kusin, Vladimir, *From Dubček to Charter '77.* Edinburgh, Scotland: Q Press, 1978.

Macartney, C. A., *Hungary: A Short History.* Edinburgh, Scotland: Edinburgh University Press, 1966.

McNally, Raymond T., and Radu Florescu, *In Search of Dracula.* Greenwich, Connecticut: New York Graphic Society, 1972.

Mikes, George, *The Hungarian Revolution.* London: Andre Deutsch, 1957.

Milosz, Czeslaw, *Portrait of Poland.* London: Thames and Hudson, 1982.

Moorhouse, Geoffrey, *Prague* (The Great Cities series). Amsterdam: Time-Life International, 1980.

Morris, L. P., *Eastern Europe since 1945.* London: Heinemann Educational Books, 1984.

Nelson, Harold D., ed., *Poland. Foreign Area Studies.* Washington, D.C.: The American University, 1984.

Oxley, Andrew, et. al., *Czechoslovakia: The Party and the People.* London: Allen Lane, 1973.

Plakot Polski (The Polish Poster). Warsaw: KAW Press, 1979.

Schonberg, Harold C., *The Lives of the Great Composers.* London: Futura Publications Limited, 1975.

Šimečka, Milan, *The Restoration of Order.* London: Verso, 1984.

Skilling, Gordon, *Charter '77 and Human Rights in Czechoslovakia.* London: George Allen & Unwin, 1981.

Steiner, Eugen, *The Slovak Dilemma.* Cambridge, England: Cambridge University Press, 1973.

Steven, Stewart, *The Poles.* London: Collins/Harvill, 1982.

Syrop, Konrad, *Poland in Perspective.* London: Robert Hale, 1982.

Tissot, Victor, *Unknown Hungary.* London: Richard Bentley and Son, 1881.

Volgyes, Ivan, *Hungary: A Nation of Contradictions.* Boulder, Colorado: Westview Press, 1982.

Walker, Alan, ed., *Franz Liszt.* London: Barrie & Jenkins, 1970.

Wallace, William V., *Czechoslovakia.* London: Ernest Benn, 1977.

PERIODICALS

Astrachan, Anthony, "The Hungarian Experience," *Connoisseur*, March 1985.

Boyes, Roger, "The New Revolution—through Evolution," *The Times*, October 15, 1984.

"Comecon Survey," *The Economist*, April 20, 1985.

"Czechoslovakia," *Financial Times* survey, October 23, 1985.

East European Reporter, Vol. 1, No. 1, London, Spring 1985.

"Hungary," *Financial Times* survey, May 14, 1985.

"Hungary: A Special Report," *The Guardian*, October 31, 1985.

Kundera, Milan, "A Kidnapped West or Culture Bows Out," *Granta*, No. 11, no date.

Momatiuk, Yva, "Poland's Mountain People," *National Geographic*, January 1981.

The New Hungarian Quarterly, Vol. 25, No. 94, Summer 1984.

"Other Heresies: Hungary," *Time*, January 6, 1986.

"Polen," *Merian*, Vol. 10, October 1982.

Putnam, John J., "Hungary's New Way," *National Geographic*, February 1983.

INDEX

Page numbers in italics indicate an illustration of the subject mentioned.